The Three-Dimensional Woman

Heather Double

New Wine Press

New Wine Press
PO Box 17
Chichester
West Sussex PO20 6YB
England

ISBN: 1 874367 48 5

Typeset by CRB Associates, Norwich
Printed in England by Clays Ltd, St Ives plc.

Acknowledgements

My heartfelt thanks goes to all those of my family and friends who have encouraged me to write this book. In particular I wish to thank Liz Reynolds, Peggy Buchanan and Tim Jones for their help in preparing the manuscript, and Cara Hines for her help with the cover design.

Dedication

This book is affectionately dedicated to my parents – John and Rhoda Martin. They taught me to love God and His Word. Thank you for your example, Mum and Dad: an example of an open heart, servanthood, and faith in God, which helped to prepare me for my own walk with God.

Contents

PART THREE
The Victorious Life of a Godly Woman 165

INTRODUCTION

As I have had the privilege of travelling with my husband in the course of our ministry, I have met women in every place who have a desire to see the fullness of God. This has been coupled with a longing to be of use to His kingdom. Both have been made clear to me not only by the questions they have asked, but also by the longing revealed in their eyes as I have talked about being able to know God. Then there are also women who have been frustrated. They know that God wants to use them but have been unable to find their 'niche' in His Church. Some of these have been drawn into the issue of women ministering and holding office in the Church. It is not my intention to speak about this subject at all. I feel that our number one emphasis in life should be that of a living, vibrant relationship with God rather than any ministry or gift.

For many years I have had a burden to write a book to try and help many of these women. I am an avid reader, and so have read most Christian books for women, and subjects associated with the life of a woman. Many of these books have frustrated me because they are written for women who are obviously married, or single, or they are aimed at women with 'problems'. It has been difficult to find a book that I could read and not feel that I was somehow different, or unique, because I had none of these 'problems'. I just wanted to read something which would develop my walk with God; feed my desire to know Him; enrich my knowledge of His Word; and give guidance on His purpose for my life, while also developing my character.

When I stand before God I stand as His child. I will not stand as my husband's wife, my child's mother, my parent's daughter, my brother's sister, or any other relationship that I have on this earth; not even a person He has given a gift or ministry to. It will not matter that I am married to one of His ministers. He will not be interested that my own children are all in His service. It will carry no weight that my parents and grandparents have been Christians. Not even that my mother was called by Him to ministry. No, I stand before God as His child and therefore I have a desire to relate to God on the basis of a Father and child relationship. When I read His word I do not put it through a filter of my husband. I read it as God's word to **me**, personally, not through an intermediary. Therefore in writing this book I am writing it for every lady who has a relationship with God as Father and Jesus Christ as their Saviour. I have not and will not make mention of a wife, or mother, sister, or daughter, or any other label. We are on our own when we stand before God and we all need to have a relationship with Him that will stand under that test. Obviously because I am married and have a family, some of the illustrations and 'life' situations I will be using will be from my own experience.

We will be looking at a considerable amount of scripture, for I uncompromisingly believe that the foundation we each need in our life is the Word of God. For many of us the Bible is not a book that we avidly read. We view it as a history book, or a book we can get advice from for a particular problem. For me the Bible is a book with God in it. It is God's word to me, personally. I believe that it is also a book for me to enjoy.

I have divided the book into three parts. These are the
three dimensions I find most women have problems with
or that there is very little written about. I have called
them:
1.   The Devotional Life of a Godly Woman.
2.   The Character of a Godly Woman.
3.   The Victorious Life of a Godly Woman.
In many ways all three are very closely linked together
and we cannot divide them, but for ease of reference and
reading I have tried to keep to the dimension we are
concerned with in each section.

The first section involves our relationship with God and
God's relationship with us. The second section concerns
how we live our life in our character towards God and
those around us. Our final section influences what comes
out of our lives, and what others see of the life of God in
our lives. So in all sections we have the inward and the
outward expression of our life. You could say that this
book is about our **upward**, **inward** and **outward** life.

We only have one life, we do not have two lives, one
human and one spiritual. After we have come to Christ,
we are one new whole being.

When ministering overseas, especially in some of the
less developed countries, we start our ministry by stating
that the principles of scripture are cross-cultural. This
means that we can take the principles of the Word of God
and work them out in our own culture, as long as the
cultural things do not violate the Word of God, and are
not sinful. I would apply this principle also to our church
'culture'. The principles of the scriptures are there for all
God's people therefore we can work them out in our personal lives no matter what church we attend. What I wish
to communicate through this book I believe applies to all
women, everywhere, wherever they live, whatever their
position, whatever their church, whatever their age or
status. God's Word is for God's children. What He has to
say to us can be applied to our own lives.

There are far too many Christians around who are

waiting for a thunderbolt from heaven to fall on them before they move into action. They are waiting for the 'prophet' of God to come and give them a 'word' before they will **do** anything for God.

Jesus said to His disciples that they were to 'go' and make disciples (Matthew 28:19). He also told them to 'go' and preach the good news to all creation (Mark 16:15). He did not say wait until I give you a call to a particular ministry, He only told them to wait for the power of the Holy Spirit to come upon them ... He just said *'Go into all the world* (Mark 16:15) ... *and be my witnesses'* (Acts 1:8). 'Be' is a doing word; it is active; it exists in the now.

The Bible tells us that we are to be salt of the earth (Matthew 5:13). Once a chef has added the salt to the recipe he is totally unaware that it is there unless he tastes it. Salt is a substance which you are oblivious of until you taste it. It is not visible once you have added it to the other ingredients. We are told by God that as Christians we are to be salt in our communities. Salt not only flavours substances but it also preserves. In our neighbourhood we are, or should be the ones who uphold the presence of godliness and holiness. Our presence should be tasted even though it is not always seen.

Jesus also told us that we must let our lights shine before men so that they will see our lives and praise God (Matthew 5:16). This is something we have to do – let our light shine. Do it naturally, because we are God's children, not because He has given us a special ministry.

We are His children therefore we can go and take the good news of the gospel. We can be His witnesses. We are salt and we can let our light shine. We don't have to wait for some 'voice from heaven' to tell us that we have been 'called' to this or that special ministry, we just 'go' and 'be'. God is not going to give us some big revelation when He has already told us what we should be doing. We have to just get on with being what God has made us to be.

Throughout the book I hope you will be asking yourself a number of questions, for it is only as we begin to look at ourselves that we can truly know where we are with God and who we are as people. It is interesting that throughout His ministry Jesus asked many people many questions which provoked them to look at themselves in a way that they had not done so before.

In the same way my desire is for us to look into our lives, ask ourselves the questions and examine our own lives in the light of God's Word.

Chapter 1

Foundations

How I Got Started

On occasions I have been asked how it all started with me, or how I came to know God. I feel I would like to tell you just a little of the way God dealt with me, and how I began my quest to know God.

I was brought up in a Christian home and taken to church every Sunday from the cradle, but it was not until I was nine years old that I can remember hearing anything about a God who was interested in me. At that time my mother was converted to Jesus Christ. She had a dynamic experience, and began searching for the truth. I can remember being taken to meetings where I saw amazing miracles of healing taking place. In some of these meetings people would come and lay hands on me and prophesy over me. One I remember very vividly. I was about 9 or 10 years old, when sometime during a meeting the preacher walked up to me and started to prophesy over me. One phrase stands out to this day – that I was going to receive a 'Double' portion of His Spirit! Needless to say this left an impression upon my life. Yes, I read my Bible, I prayed, I went to church (sometimes as often as three times on a Sunday, plus nearly every night of the week), sang in the choir and became a Sunday school teacher, yet in spite of all this, it was not until I was 15 years old that Jesus became a real person to me. I had been doing all the right things, attending every meeting which I was physically able to, responding to many altar calls in my search for God, but it was not until this time that Jesus became a reality in my own life. Yes, I had known God answer prayer for me many times, but I can only say that I know what happened to me at this time, and it was very different to anything I had known before, and to me it was the time when my walk with God really began.

During this time I was filled with the Holy Spirit and suddenly, overnight, the Bible became a book which was alive. I began to read it, not casually but zealously. I can remember times when I could not put it down I was so absorbed in what I was reading.

It was also at this time that a boldness came into my life which was not there before. I had a desire to tell others what I had received and so I obtained some gospel tracts and spent much of my free time on the streets witnessing. One very memorable event took place around this time.

One Saturday my friend and I were witnessing to some young merchant seamen at one of our local fishing ports. As you can imagine, two young sixteen-year old girls witnessing to hardened seamen were laughed at and ridiculed. That was not the end though. The next day, Sunday, saw my friend and I at our local church. We were totally taken by surprise when one of these young seamen came into church! He sat through the meeting and at the end asked if he could say something. We wondered what he was going to say. He told us that after we had witnessed to him he and his mates had a good laugh. Later on they went into the pub and ordered their usual tipple, but as he went to take his first sip the face of Jesus appeared over the tankard! He threw it across the bar, ran home, got by on his knees by his bed, repented of his sin and was born-again! At that time this meant a lot to me, especially in the light of what was to happen over the next few months.

It was through the searching of the scriptures, that a

13

year later I felt God call me to give my job up and serve Him full-time. This was confirmed to me often through the reading of His Word, but also through other ways.

All Change

One day a young preacher came to our home in search of his friend, who was the pastor of our church. Because his friend was away that day and it was our mid-week Bible Study night, he was asked to take the meeting.

I will never forget that message; it was to change the direction of my life! He took the scripture from John 14:15 *'If you love me, you will obey what I command.'* I knew once again that God was telling me that one of His commands to me was full-time service.

Next day I gave in my notice and starting serving God. I knew only one thing, that I was being obedient to what I felt God was telling me. I did not know where or what I would be doing; only that I was being obedient. I also felt very strongly that God had a specific call on me to the ministry of helps. We read of this in 1 Corinthians 12:28. I really did not know what this meant.

Then one day while reading the story of Abraham and how God called him to leave his home and travel to another land, I somehow felt that God would have me travelling, so with my last wage packet I bought a suitcase (it actually cost me my whole wage packet).

Three years later I was married to that young preacher who visited our church that eventful day. Yes, it was my husband, Don. I believe God has a sense of humour! Remember I told you about the prophecy over me that I would have a double portion of His Spirit? Now I had changed my name to Double! That night changed not only my life but also my name. Since then I have travelled to over 40 countries with my husband, helping him wherever and whenever and however possible. How grateful I am that I began my walk with God searching for the truth, seeking to know what God had for me as a woman in His kingdom, working out my own relationship with Him and being obedient to what I felt He was saying to me. So you can see why it is I believe so strongly that we need this foundation of the Word of God in our lives.

Different is not Wrong

In Philippians 2:12 Paul tells us to continue to work out our own salvation with fear and trembling. There is no way that we can literally 'work out our own salvation', for Jesus purchased our salvation when He died and rose again, but there is an area in which each one of us have to work out our own relationship with God.

Working out our own walk with God means that we have no props. It will also mean that each one of us will have a very different relationship with God. Because I met God in a different way from you does not mean that one of those ways is wrong. Because I have had to prove God in different areas of life from you will mean that I will have a different perspective of God's character and personality. Therefore my relationship with God will probably come from a different viewpoint than yours. Some of us will know God as a loving, caring Father, because of what He has delivered us from; others will know Him as a tough God of justice. Our aspect of God will also vary because of the gifts and calling He has placed upon our lives. Someone called to minister to those in prisons will know God as the one who looks beyond the faults and failings and sees the need. Some who are called to alleviate suffering will know the God who comforts, heals and brings freedom from bondage. Those who are called to a pastoral ministry will know the God who cares for the inner person. One called to evangelism will know the God who forgives and loves the sinner. One who knows the God who moves His people into action will usually be called to some kind of social action. So none of us must condemn another because they relate to God and see Him from a different perspective.

I came to realise very early in my marriage that my husband could be taken from me at any time. Travelling as he did, all over the world, by every mode of transport available meant I could be a widow at any time. Therefore I needed to develop my own walk with God, my own faith, my own salvation. I required an ability to hear God speak to me personally. I needed to be able to search the scriptures for myself. I could not rely upon my husband always to be there to bolster my faith, pray for me, pick me up off the floor or anything else, so I sought God for myself. I began to work out my own salvation, and I believe that this is what we all need to do as children of God.

I have endeavoured to cover areas which I have sought God on for my own life; things I have worked out for myself, subjects which I have had my own personal battles with. My desire is that each one of you will be taken deeper into your relationship with God as a result.

I want us to start by laying aside our status in life. Forget that you are a wife, a mother, a sister, a daughter; that you are widowed, single, a single parent, or whatever label we place upon ourselves.

Chapter 2

Beginnings

Beginnings are very important. How we start something will often affect how we continue. I never had a blinding light, a sudden dramatic, overnight revelation; and often during my pursuit of God I have felt unsure of my salvation because I had not had that kind of experience. I have faced the fact that I did not, and sought God in order to have the full assurance of faith we read of in Hebrews 10:22. There is one thing I am sure of, and that is that I do know God as my Father, and I have a relationship with Jesus Christ as my Saviour. I also have an on-going experience of the moving of the Holy Spirit in my life.

Many people whom I have met have had dynamic experiences, my own husband being one of them. No matter how you came to start your relationship with God, the one important fact that you should know with certainty, is that you are a child of God. If you do not, then you can.

Often when preaching the gospel we readily declare that God has no grandchildren! In relationship to God we are all children. Because our parents and perhaps grand-parents were born again believers, it is not an automatic follow-on that we are also Christians. Sometimes when giving my testimony I will use the verse from Matthew 5:20 that says – *'unless your righteousness surpasses that of the Pharisees and the teachers of the law, you will certainly*

17

not enter the kingdom of heaven.' This means that our righteousness has to come directly from God Himself, not from something that we do ourselves (Romans 3:22; Romans 4:5; Romans 5:17).

Please note, this righteousness does not come by our praying much, good works, Bible study, church-going or anything else. It comes only through faith in Jesus Christ. Because I was involved in the traditions and trappings of what had been the outward show of a Christian life before I had my personal encounter with Jesus Christ, it did not mean that I did not have to come the same way as everyone else. Jesus said that He was the way to God (John 14:6). The first step we have to take is to come to God the Father through Jesus Christ. The next step we find in Acts 2:38, when Peter said we must repent. In order to repent we need to acknowledge that we have sinned. When many of us have been brought up in Christian homes, it is sometimes difficult for us to admit that we have sinned. We look at others who have been redeemed from some of the most terrible lives of sin and we almost feel that we are clean compared with them. David said *'Surely I was sinful at birth, sinful from the time my mother conceived me'* (Psalm 51:5). David had a godly mother and father; he was one of the chosen people of God; but he still said that from birth he was sinful. He acknowledged the fact that ever since Adam and Eve fell in the Garden of Eden and yielded to Satan's temptation, man has been born in sin.

When the Bible records that God made man and woman we are told that He made them in His own image. God made us in His image which was divine, spotlessly clean, no sin. After Adam sinned it was impossible for him to reproduce his kind in the same way as he was created, pure and without sin. In Genesis 5:3 we read than when Adam had lived one hundred and thirty years, he had a son in his own likeness, in his own image; and he named him Seth. What does it mean 'in his own likeness'? I believe it means that Seth was born like Adam was then, sinful, without God in his life. Adam was no longer divine in his nature, he was now a sinner, he had the sentence of death in his body. God said to Adam and Eve that they were not to eat of the tree of the knowledge of good and evil, for if they did they would die (Genesis 2:16–17). From the moment that Adam and Eve ate of the fruit of the tree of the knowledge of good and evil they began to die. Therefore everyone who has been born since, has been born in the likeness of his ancestors with the sentence of death on his life. We all need then to repent of that sinful nature. Even if we have only done what we may think is a little sin, we still need to have the nature of sin dealt with in our lives, and this can only be done by repenting and turning to God. It saddens my heart when I hear the Gospel preached without any mention of repentance, for the Bible is very clear on the subject. In Luke 13:5 Jesus said '... *unless you repent, you too will all perish.*'

Repentance was one of the things that made a great difference in my walk with God. Many times when I responded to 'altar calls' for various things I shed tears, often not in repentance but because I had no assurance that God had accepted me. I knew so much in my head, but felt nothing in my heart! It was not until I had truly repented that I had any assurance that God had accepted me and that I was His child. Because of living a very 'closed' life in 'the church', with all my Christian friends, my faith had not been challenged. I had no dramatic change that gave me any evidence that I was a new creature, but when I had truly repented then there came an assurance that I had not known before. This was so vital for me. I recollect one preacher who regularly preached on what he termed a 'Christian' repentance. Repentance is not something that we do only when we first acknowledge that we are a sinner and need a saviour. Repentance should become an attitude of life for the Christian.

As I have travelled I have come to realise that the word 'Christian' in many areas only means that you do not belong to another religion. In no way does it mean that one is born-again, knowing God as their Father and Jesus as their personal Saviour. I recall one time having to explain to some people who were visiting a foreign country with us that when our driver said he was a 'Christian' it did not mean that he knew Jesus as we did. It was very hard for them to understand. Being reared in Britain, they were brought with the idea that when someone said they were a Christian it meant that they had made Jesus Christ the Lord of their life.

Water baptism was another big step for me. It gave me an assurance that my old life had been dealt with and that I was now a new creation (Romans 6:4–7). Once we have had a real personal encounter with Jesus Christ and we have that assurance that we are children of God then we can start on the road to knowing God.

PART ONE

The Devotional Life
of a Godly Woman

Chapter 3

What Is Devotion?

First let us answer the question of what is meant by the term 'devotional life'.

Most likely it will mean something quite different to each one of us. Usually it means a 'quiet time' when we are alone, and we read the Word of God and pray. How, where, and when this will happen, can vary with each one of us. The important point is that we do have a devotional life. By this I mean that we have an intimate relationship with God.

What constitutes that relationship will be different for each of us. As I said before 'different is not wrong'. We have to work out our own salvation and relationship with God (Philippians 2:12).

Often when I am studying the Word of God I look up words in a dictionary to discover the depth of the word. I did this with 'devotion' and this is what I discovered:
 - to have an earnest zeal in the performance of religious duties and ceremonies;
 - an act of prayer or supplication;
 - ardent love or affection for;
 - a strong attachment to;
 - prayers or service of worship.

I believe all of these should be a description of our devotional life with God. Yet when we use the word these definitions are really the furthest from our minds. If any, perhaps the last one comes fairly close. The devotional life for many Christians is a time when they quickly read a passage of scripture before they start their day. For some, who find it difficult to get up early in the morning, it will be a time when they come home at the end of the day, or just before they go to sleep, or at some other convenient time.

A devotional life should be far more than this, for I believe it is a life-style. From my study of scripture I am convinced that our relationship with God should be just that; a life-style and not just a so-called 'QT' (Quiet Time).

First of all our devotion should be whole-hearted. For many people their 'QT' is far from being whole-hearted. They rush to see how quickly they can get through it. 2 Kings 20:3 and 1 Chronicles 28:9 give us this thought of a whole-hearted devotion to God. Solomon tells us that he served with a willing mind.

When we are whole-hearted in our devotion to God there is no room for us to be devoted to anything else. Otherwise we will fall into the trap that Jesus spoke of, when trying to serve two masters, which is impossible. We end up hating one (Matthew 6:24).

Our devotional life should not be a hit-and-miss situation. It should be consistent. Because of the pace of our lives today and also the uncertainty that many of us live in, especially those of us who are involved in Christian work in some way, to be consistent is hard when we are only thinking about a certain time, or specified length of time, or a certain place that constitutes our devotional life.

A devotional life can be visual, something that other people can see. The best example for us is from Daniel 6:10–13. Daniel's devotion to God was so visual that everybody knew about it. He opened his windows and prayed. Even when he knew that he was going to be summoned before the King he still did it quite openly. His devotion to God was so strong that he was willing not just to be seen to pray to God, but also to be judged for it.

23

Through his devotion he had become so familiar with his God, that he knew He would not let him down. It was truly inconvenient for Daniel to be thrown into the lion's den, yet for us our devotional life has to fit into our convenience; when it pleases us. It is usually hidden in our home, and even then when family and friends are around, it often means in our own room. There is nothing wrong with this, but it should not just be confined to this.

There is a place for both; the open, visible devotion to God and also the hidden life with God. Jesus made this very clear in Matthew 6:6 when he told us that when we pray, we should go into our room, close the door and pray to our Father, who is unseen. Then our Father, who sees what is done in secret, will reward us openly. We can see there is a place for balance to be brought into our devotional life. We should be known to be a people of devotion to God by our visible devotion, but we should also have a place where we pray and commune with God privately.

Because communion with God is two-way there are scriptures that tell us certain things we can expect from God. David asks God to guard his life because he is devoted to Him (Psalm 86:2). There are many other things that we can expect from God, things which the Bible tells us are ours. Here are just three:

- **His love**   (Romans 5:8; Romans 8:35–39)
- **His care**   (1 Peter 5:7; Ephesians 5:29)
- **His commitment in relationship**   (Hebrews 13:5; Matthew 28:20)

There are also many times when the Bible calls God our Father (Luke 11:13; Luke 12:32; Matthew 6:8). One of the main passages which expresses that our devotion to God should be total, continual and a life-style, comes from Deuteronomy 6:4–9. It tells us to love the Lord our God with all our heart, soul and strength; that His Word (commandments) should be in our heart; that we must impress them on our children; talk about them when we are home, on the road, on our bed; we are to use them as symbols on our hands and forehead; we are to write them

24

on the doorframes of our house and on our gates. This gives quite extensive instruction on the how and the where and when of our devotional life. This is one of the many scriptures that teach us that our devotion to God is a lifestyle more than something we do just out of duty.

Chapter 4

Prayer

Matthew 6:6 gives us some guidelines when we come
to prayer. Let us look at the five main points from this
verse:

(a) When you pray – this indicates that there should be a
    time in our devotional life with God when we do actu-
    ally have a time of prayer, or direct communion with
    God.

(b) Go into your room – there is an indication here that
    there can be a place where we find it easier to pray. It
    may be a room, a certain chair or place, a particular
    spot in the garden or a place where we enjoy walking.
    (One of my favourite places is by the sea.)

(c) Close the door – here we have the thought that we
    need to pray alone, and shut the world out of our
    minds, and life.

(d) Reward you openly – there will be visible evidence
    that we have a vital prayer life with God.

A little further on Jesus says that we should pray in this
manner:

'Our Father in heaven, hallowed be your name.'
                                            (Matthew 6:9)

(1) *Our* – indicates it is a personal relationship.
(2) *Father* – gives us an authority figure to approach.

(3) *Heaven* – is the place where God dwells, above where we live.

(4) *Hallowed* – there is a recognition of reverence.

Our communication with God therefore must be personal, we must positively address a person in authority. There needs to be an acknowledgement that He is the King of kings, Lord of lords and Sovereign, and that He is higher than all others, and there must be godly fear and awesomeness in approaching a holy God.

Prayer is a direction of our thoughts and our feelings towards God.

Jesus also gave us instruction on how we should pray. We have had many sermons preached and many books written about the prayer that Jesus used as an example for our prayer life. This prayer is commonly called 'The Lord's Prayer', but He gave us much more instruction than just that one instance.

His own prayer life with God His Father is our example. He told us that when we pray, we should not keep on babbling like pagans. They think they will be heard because of their many words. I believe this means that we must not use long-winded prayers when we communion with God, but we must pray what is on our hearts and then listen to God, because He is not going to hear us just because we pray long prayers. When we listen to how the pagans, or perhaps today we would call them cults, pray using mantras which are often the name of one of their gods repeated over and over, we begin to see what Jesus was saying.

Relationship is more important than lots of words spoken with no reality of relationship with God. Jesus also uses an example from His own Jewish culture to teach us about prayer.

A very popular verse that is often quoted in prayer meetings, is Matthew 18:19–20. This says that where *'two or three come together in my name there am I with them.'* It is interesting that Jesus said this because His own culture taught that before you could pray, except in your own communion with God, there had to be a gathering of ten men, called a *'minyan'*. Any male who had experienced his bar-mitzvah was eligible to be part of this group. What Jesus was really saying here, was that you do not have to wait for ten to gather. You can pray and commune with God whenever you wish to. In effect He was saying that we could approach God at any time. He was looking forward to the day when He knew that the veil in the temple would be split in two from top to bottom. The Holy of Holies would be open for everyone to enter into and not just the High Priest (Matthew 27:51; Mark 15:38; Luke 23:45). For a full understanding of this point we need to read through the book of Hebrews, especially chapters nine and ten.

Hebrews 10:19–22 tells us that we can approach God with confidence when we know that we have been cleansed by the blood of the Lord Jesus Christ from our sin.

Paul tells us something that is quite revolutionary in 1 Thessalonians 5:17. He instructs us to *'pray continually'*. How can we pray continually? Probably most of us would say that this is impossible, particularly if all we think about prayer is that it must be in a certain place, at a certain time, in a certain way. No, to pray continually just means that we have a relationship with God and can approach and talk to Him at any given moment. In fact, whenever we have a need to talk to Him we can approach Him. This I believe, is 'a devotional life'.

When perhaps a member of your family or a close friend has been away, have you ever felt the need to talk to them? There is just something that you need to communicate to them; not just a piece of gossip but something from yourself, from your heart, openly and frankly. So what we usually do, is pick up the 'phone to call them and communicate. This is really what Jesus and Paul were saying. Whenever we need to we can communicate with our Father God.

In the human realm if we want to communicate intimately with someone we usually have something in common with them. We have a topic or subject that begins our communication. When my children became teenagers I soon discovered that I needed a new communication level with them. Childish toys were no longer relevant. There was a need to discover a new way of communicating. So I began to show some interest in things that I really had not much knowledge about. Sports, computers, pop music, and various other teenage interests. The things we should have in common with God are things like, His Son, the Holy Spirit, His Word, His people.

Getting to know His Son and the Holy Spirit will bring us in touch with God.

Living in His kingdom will bring us into the realm where He dwells. Building relationships with His church will give us a positive communication topic.

Using His Word as our counsellor will give us the language with which to communicate with Him.

Rubbing shoulders with His people will give us the same kind of friendships He has.

So often we get offended at God because our prayers are not answered, and the reason is that one of these basic elements is missing. The prophet Amos asks a very pertinent question on this subject:

> *'Do two walk together unless they have agreed to do so?'* (Amos 3:3)

Can we really expect God to walk with us if we are not in agreement about the same things?

Jesus told his disciples a parable in order to show them that they should always pray and not give up (Luke 18:1). We need perseverance in prayer. Jesus gave us a parable that clearly teaches us this point (Luke 11:5–10). He told of a man whose friend comes to him at midnight and doesn't give up until he gets an answer.

If we only think of prayer as something we do with our eyes closed, then this type of prayer will be impossible to us. A hymn written by James Montgomery expresses the essence of prayer perfectly:

> Prayer is the soul's sincere desire,
> Uttered or unexpressed,
> The motion of a hidden fire,
> That trembles in the breast.
>
> Prayer is the burden of a sigh,
> The falling of a tear,
> The upward glancing of an eye,
> When none but God is near.

Judson Cornwall says:

> 'Prayer is a personal activity, it is not a spectator sport. Listening to another pray is not prayer. Prayer is personal communication.'

Just as prayer is a continual attitude of having an open line through to God at any time, so is our devotional life. It is hard to separate our devotional life from our prayer life, for when our devotional life is a live communion with God, prayer becomes a vital part of that life-style. 'Prayer meetings' and praying with prayer partners, or praying for specific needs, become an on-going part of our life. When our prayer life becomes an extension of ourselves, we won't have to suddenly go into an 'attitude of prayer' when we come upon a problem that needs God's intervention. We are on 'talking terms' with God. To be on talking terms means that we have a relationship with Him. We can come into His presence and make a request any time we wish.

I heard of an incident which happened when John Kennedy was president of the USA. During his term of office it was not unusual to see his children freely walking around the White House. One day someone observed a child walking through the corridors with none of the security guards taking any notice of it. This continued until the child actually got to the Oval Office door. The child was not stopped. It went through the door, walked into the office, approached the President, climbed onto his lap and stayed there while the President continued his work. Why did the child do that? Because it knew who its father was, and it knew that it had access at any time to its father. What a clear picture of how our relationship with God should work. Prayer is all about relationships.

There are many things that can hinder our devotional life. Let us consider the life of Job. Job had his friends. 'Job's comforters' is a modern day idiom. They were not a real help to Job. They distracted him. Job told them that they even undermined his piety and hindered his devotion to God (Job 15:4). Nothing was going to make Job think anything less of his God. He knew that God knew all about him. In Job 23:10 he declared that God knew the way he took, and when God had tested him then he would come forth as gold. His devotion to God was pure and his friends were not going to be allowed to divert him.

For us today it may not be our friends, but our family, our possessions, our position in our career, our work mates and our college peers that try and hinder our devotion to God. Paul also says that he was afraid that the Corinthians may be led astray from their devotion to Christ by deception (2 Corinthians 11:3). This can be the same for us today. With all the modern false doctrines, cults, New Age, and other philosophies around we could so easily fall into deception and be led astray.

It would be simple in today's culture to allow our devotion to God to become cold and lifeless. Instead of getting better it appears to worsen the longer we walk with God. Communion with God is two-way. Not just us talking to God but also God talking to us. Many people say to me that they do not know when God is speaking to them, or they cannot hear God's voice. Jesus had something to say about this in John 10:1–5. He tells us that the sheep follow their shepherd because they know his voice.

31

Each one of us should be able to recognise our Shepherd's voice. It is something that we need to train ourselves in, so that we know when it is God speaking to us. Some say they do not know if it is God, Satan or themselves. They just do not know the difference. Only we can train ourselves to recognise our Shepherd's voice.

If we desire to know the will of God for our lives then it is imperative that we cultivate a good prayer communion with our Heavenly Father. For it is only as we have a direct line of communication with Him that we will be able to know what His will is for us.

Jesus told his disciples that He could do nothing by Himself, He could do only what He saw His Father doing (John 5:19–20). Prayer will give us a clear vision and will also direct our path in the ways of God.

The greater the pressure of our day, the greater the need for prayer. Busyness is a poor excuse for prayer**less**ness, but a good reason for prayer**ful**ness. I believe the busier we are going to be the more prayerful we should be. For it is only in communion with God that we will know His strength to complete all that we have to do for Him. Many times in the Gospels we read statements about Jesus' prayer life:

> *'A great while before it was day . . . '* (Mark 1:35)

> *'. . . He rose early and went to a solitary place to pray.'* (Mark 1:35)

> *'Jesus went up the mountain on his own to pray.'* (Matthew 14:23)

Jesus' life teaches us that when we are busy for God we must also be busy in prayer.

Chapter 5

Have We Met God?

In the Bible we have a number of incidents when God met people. Sometimes the people were not even seeking Him, yet God still met them. Whenever we meet God we can be sure of one thing, that there will be a change in our lives. No one can meet God and not be changed.

We read in Exodus 33:11 that the Lord said He was going to meet Moses face to face, as a man speaks with his friend. God was going to have an intimate relationship with Moses. When you speak face to face with someone, you meet them 'eye-ball to eye-ball'. You are open with them, you hold nothing back from them. You share your heart with them. This was what God said He was going to do with Moses. We then read in Exodus 34:33–34 that the result of this meeting with God meant that Moses put a veil over his face. Why did he have to cover his face after speaking with God? Because his face was changed, it shone with the presence and glory of the Lord and the people could not bear to look at Moses.

When we meet God there will always be evidence that we have met Him – that evidence will be a change in our lives. It may be internal or it may be external for all to see, but there will always be evidence that we have truly met with God.

When Saul met the Lord on the road to Damascus in Acts 9, we are told that suddenly a light from heaven flashed around him. Saul fell to the ground and heard a voice speak to him. The men travelling with Saul stood there speechless because they heard the voice but did not see anyone. When Saul got up from the ground, he was blind. As a result of this encounter with God Saul was changed; his name was changed, his career was changed, his whole life was changed. Yet the people with Saul heard God but could not see anything.

One of the most important things in our devotional life is a meeting with God. I believe that when we have a real meeting with God then our devotional life takes on new meaning for us.

Each one of Jesus' disciples had a changed life because of meeting Him. I believe that when we meet with God we will also have a life-changing experience.

The first change is that we are no longer citizens of this dark world but we have become citizens of the kingdom of God (Ephesians 5:8; Colossians 1:13). After our initial meeting with God, that of repenting and receiving salvation, we need to continue to meet with God regularly. At times there will be a very definite result of that meeting. At other times it will be just an on-going relationship that we find replenishes us but there will always be something that we can tangibly talk about. We can never have a real encounter with God and not have something happen.

God will speak to us about various things in our lives. Because we are not yet perfect there will always be things that God will need to change in us. I can look back on my walk with God and know things He has said to me and how I have been changed, but I know that there is still much more to be done in me.

Things God will say to us should always change us; change the way we think, the way we talk, the way we live and what we believe. No one can really meet God and not be affected.

In our devotional life it is important that we have meetings – yes, plural – meetings with God. Throughout our lives there will be times when we are in need of a new encounter with Him, we will feel a thirst for a new meeting with God, a fresh revelation of who He is.

In Psalm 42:1–2 David expresses his desire as a thirst for God. Jesus told us in His famous Sermon on the Mount that we are blessed when we hunger and thirst after righteousness (Matthew 5:6). He also told us that if we are thirsty, when we come to Him our thirst will be quenched (John 7:37). One thing is certain, that if we have a hunger and a thirst for God then He will satisfy us (Psalm 107:9).

One of the evidences of a devotional life that is really working will be that we come to know God. Jesus' prayer in John 17:3 expresses this point. He says that eternal life is that we many know the only true God **and** Jesus Christ.

It appears to me that the majority of Christians today talk a great deal about their relationship with Jesus Christ to the point of leaving God out. Yet the very reason that Jesus Christ came to this earth was in order that we can be reconciled back to God (Ephesians 2:16; Colossians 1:20; 2 Corinthians 5:18). Christ's death upon the Cross, His burial in the tomb and His resurrection are not ends in themselves. Although they are the central point of the Gospel they can only have reality and substance as we put them in relationship to God's prior revelation of Himself to mankind. The very reason God created man was in order to have a relationship with Him. God sent His Son to redeem mankind so that He could once again relate to mankind. The communion had been broken because of sin.

When we commune with God there is a need for it to be more than just need-centred. If God only exists to meet our needs then He is nothing more than a Santa Claus, Fairy Godmother, or even a Genie who can produce anything we desire at the flick of a wrist! No, our relationship with God rests upon something much deeper than just meeting our needs. It is a deep communion, an intimate, heart-felt desire to know Him and to love Him.

Whatever or whoever we love will motivate us. The

greater our knowledge of God the greater our love for Him, and vice-versa. If we do not seek our love in God Himself then we will be sure to seek it elsewhere, because God had made mankind with the emotions of being loved and loving.

Paul's whole life and his epistles are dedicated to the mission of bringing people into a knowledge of God. In Ephesians 1:17 Paul tells us that he keeps on asking that we will have the Spirit of wisdom and revelation, so that we may know Him better. A revelation of who God is will start us on the road to loving Him, for anyone who you love, you will desire to get to know. I have never yet met a young lady who has begun to feel true love for a young man who has not tried to get to know the young man. Good relationships are built when people desire to have a knowledge of the other person, not just an acquaintanceship. We all have many of this type of relationship with people we know only a little, but a good relationship has to be built on a knowledge of the other person. This is how we must also view our relationship with God. Having a desire to know God will start with a love for Him (1 John 5:20). A test to know whether we know God or not is to see if we are being obedient to His commands, not just the written ones we have in the Bible but also those He has spoken to us' personally (1 John 2:4; 1 John 4:8). We will never be able to get to know God until we start with loving Him. Our security needs to come from our **relationship** with God, before we seek it in **activity** for God. There are many people around today who find their joy and security in what they do for God rather than in their relationship to God. These people need to know who God is to them and who they are to God. We cannot confess to know God until we have become obedient to what He has said to us.

In Philippians 3:8–10 Paul expressed that his one ambition in life was to serve his God better than he had already. What a statement, especially when we consider what Paul had already accomplished in his life. We cannot really tell how many churches he had planted. He had travelled and seen the then known world. Yet all of this counted as nothing because of his consuming desire to know God better. Intimacy with his God was Paul's passion in life. On the road to Damascus, his life had been totally changed from one of hostility towards God and God's people, to one of intimacy and knowing God.

Although we may never be able to know God perfectly at least we can all have the heart-felt desire to know God better than we do at present. We enter into this intimacy with God by faith. Believing that God wants to know us, accepting the fact that God has done all that He can do to make Himself available to us through Jesus Christ, we simply respond to God. He waits for us to say like Paul did: I want to know You God: I want to know the power of the resurrection of Jesus Christ: I want to know the fellowship of His suffering: I want to be like Him.

The modern day psalmist, wanting to deepen his understanding and knowledge of God, put it this way – 'I want to know You, Lord, much more than I do.' I wonder just how often we have sung these words but not really prayed them from our hearts!

Chapter 6

Hearing God's Voice

Many people come to me and say that they do not know God's voice speaking to them. Sometimes I ask the question – 'What was the last thing He said to you?' and 'Have you done what He told you to do on that occasion?' The answer quite often is 'No!' Then I ask them how they expect God to say anything else to them until they have first done the last thing He told them to do! Obedience is a good way forward in hearing God's voice. When we are born again and filled with the Holy Spirit we have the Spirit of God dwelling within us. It is this same Spirit that will teach us to hear the voice of God.

There are many other reasons why we do not hear God's voice. I want to look at a few Bible characters. The first one is Mary. Have you ever wondered why, when Mary came to the tomb on that first resurrection morning, she did not recognise Jesus, but thought that He was the gardener? (John 20). I would submit to you that perhaps the main reason was her grief. She was so distraught at the thought that Jesus had died and now even His body had been removed, that her grief prevented her from recognising Him.

I would think that most people who read this book will one day, if not already, face grief. There are various things that we can grieve over. At one time I was under the impression that grief was only to do with people dying. At that time the only people who had died who were close to me were my grandparents. They were all Christians. Two of them were well over ninety years old when they died, so there was really no grief involved. During one of our summer camps someone said to me that they sensed I was grieving. I could not relate to it, but because I respected the person I accepted it, and put it on a shelf believing that God would show me this at a later date. About 18 months later, I was attending my own local church when God showed me very clearly what I was grieving about; not because of death but over broken relationships. Ever since we started our ministry, my husband and I have headed up an evangelistic team. At times we have had as many as 40 full-time workers. I had been through the experience of having people leave the team, for various reasons, some causing much pain. Also we had just been through a painful phase in our home-church. Some people had left, people who I was quite close to. I had a very close relationship with a few of them, and I was grieving because of those broken relationships. I had built up a wall around me, not allowing anyone else to get close to me. I had hardened my heart, because I did not want to be hurt again. That morning I allowed God to deal with the grief. About three months later I met someone I had not seen for a long while and after being with them a few minutes they said to me – 'What has happened to you? You are much softer!' I was able to tell them and it was a joy to be able to open my life and allow them to come close. Grief will not only stop us relating to people but it will also stop us from hearing God.

During this time in my life I had come to the place where I found it difficult to hear God. I had grown cold in my walk with Him, and was no longer enjoying my devotional life. Perhaps you find yourself in a similar state in your walk with God? Then take a few moments to allow Him to deal with grief. Jesus took our grief upon the cross so that we would not have to bear it (Isaiah 53:4). Most modern translations of the Bible uses the word *'sorrows'*, but older versions use the word *'grief'*. No matter which word you use, the sentiments are the same, and Jesus bore them for us. Give them to Him so that you can begin a fresh walk with God today.

After Jesus had been crucified and resurrected we read that the disciples went back to their fishing (John 21:4–7). Verse 4 tells us that Jesus stood on the shore, but His disciples did not realise it was Him. He began to speak to them, but still they did not recognise Him. It was not until He performed a miracle and they caught the load of fishes that Peter recognised Him. Throwing off his coat Peter ran to Him.

Why did the disciples not recognise Jesus when He stood on the shore? They had lived with Him for more than three years, and been involved with Him intimately, yet they did not recognise Him! I would suggest to you that the reason was disappointment (Acts 1:6). The disciples, all good Jews, were looking for the Messiah to come who they knew would be bringing in a new Kingdom and they believed Jesus was the Messiah. They thought that the Kingdom was going to be a physical kingdom and that it had to do with Israel. They were disappointed that this had not happened, so they had gone back to the only thing they knew how to do – fishing. This also proved to be very disappointing. It would seem that they had forgotten how to fish, for they had caught nothing! Then this person appeared on the shore, not unusual I suppose, but you would have thought they would have noticed that it was Jesus. He had to do what they knew Him best for, which was working miracles. He told them to put the net down again on the right side of the boat and when they caught the fish, they then recognised that it was Jesus.

Disappointment can cause us not to hear God's voice. So many of us become disappointed when God does not answer our prayers just **as** we desired Him to; or **when** we wanted Him to. We begin then to feel that we can no longer trust Him. Our disappointment leads us to close our hearts off from Him, which means we do not hear Him. Romans 5:5 tells us that hope does not disappoint us, because God has poured His love into our hearts by the Holy Spirit. The psalmist says that when we trust in God we will not be disappointed (Psalms 22:5). Isaiah then tells us that when we know God, and place our hope in Him we will not be disappointed (Isaiah 49:23). If you feel that you have become disappointed in people, or even in God Himself, then begin to rebuild your trust in Him and allow Him to take away the disappointment. We often only have disappointment because we have prayed for something and it has not happened just when and how we wanted it to. We begin to think that God does not love us, and we allow the devil to make us feel disappointed. Let God take that disappointment and allow Him to fill you with His love so you can start to trust Him again.

In Luke 24:13–16, and 30–31 we have the account of two of Jesus' disciples walking along the road to Emmaus. Jesus draws alongside, walks with them, discusses the scriptures and talks about events around them, yet they did not recognise Him. In verses 14–15 we see that they were preoccupied with the circumstances around them. They were talking about all that had happened in the last few days. Their involvement with events around them had caused them to be blinded to Jesus' presence with them.

I feel that today we can become so involved with our own activities that we miss the presence of the Lord when He draws near to commune with us. Church activities are very good and we should all be as much involved with our churches as we can. But these very activities can still be a hindrance to us in recognising the presence of the Lord. They can also hinder us from hearing His voice.

In Luke 14:15–24 we have the story of the parable of the banquet. Three of the men invited to the feast were so involved with their own affairs that they missed the banquet. The things that they were preoccupied with were all very legitimate things. One had bought a field and he needed to go and view it. Another had purchased a pair of

41

oxen and needed to prove them. The other had married a wife. What could these three things represent in our lives today? The field speaks to us of property, the oxen perhaps a new car, and marriage is still the same. We need to be sure that we do not become so preoccupied with things in our lives that we miss obeying God's invitation to communion with Him. There is no valid excuse for us missing God.

I am convinced that some people cannot hear God's voice because they are continually looking for signs and wonders. Jesus had some strong words to say to the Pharisees and teachers of the law who came to Him asking for signs (Matthew 12:38–39). He told them that only a wicked and adulterous generation asks for a miraculous sign! (Matthew 16:1–4; Luke 11:16; John 6:30). These types of people are always looking for God to manifest Himself to them by some miraculous sign and they cannot hear the still small voice of God. In the book of 1 Kings 19:11–12 we have the incident when Elijah was hidden in the cleft in the rock and God passed by. There were earthquake, wind, and fire, but God was not in any of these. Then came a still small whisper and it was God's voice. God wants us to hear His voice in the stillness. He does not always want us to see Him manifest Himself in miraculous signs and wonders. When we have a true relationship with God we will be able to hear and recognise God's voice however and wherever and whenever He speaks.

In 1 Samuel 3:1–10 we have the very well-known story of God calling Samuel. It is a story that most of us probably heard at a very early age. It is used quite often as an illustration that children can hear God speaking to them. I want us to look at this story from a very different angle. Have you ever stopped to think, just why did Samuel miss the voice as being the voice of God?

Samuel had been brought up in the temple from the day he had been weaned. He had become very familiar with the routine of the temple, and had most probably, because

42

of Eli's age, become very used to being called for various reasons. When he heard this voice his first thought was that it must be Eli, for there was no one else in the temple. In other words he had become so familiar with the routine of the temple and his own orders of service, that he did not stop to think that it could have been someone else. Certainly not God.

We need to look at our own lives and ask ourselves this question. Have the things of God become so familiar to me that I miss hearing God's voice speak to me?

We can become so familiar with the way our church does things; the hymns and choruses which we sing, or even the sermons that we hear preached, and we really do miss God's voice. Samuel needed someone else to tell him that the voice he was hearing was God's voice. Have we become so caught up with the routine of our spiritual life that we need someone else to tell us that we are hearing God's voice?

Years ago I had a friend who had been through Bible School. He graduated as one of their top students, had become a Pastor and successfully led two large churches. Then one day he realised that the ministry was meaning far more to him than Jesus Christ Himself. As a result for one whole year he sat in his own congregation and did no ministry, until Jesus meant more to him than ministry! Yes, even the ministry can become so familiar to us that we miss out in our personal devotional walk with God.

It is only in our 'vertical' relationship, with God, that we will find what we need to give in the 'horizontal' plane of ministry to others.

In all probability there are those of you reading this that feel the last two points, that of being pre-occupied, or becoming over-familiar with the things of God, apply to your lives. If so, take a while just now to reassess your values and re-establish your relationship with God.

When we make our ministry or service on the horizontal plane, we tend to gauge how we are doing spiritually by

43

looking at our gift of natural energy and thinking that is what God desires, rather than an anointing upon a life.

Jeremiah 9:23–24 says that we are allowed to boast about nothing else but that we know God. When we begin to realise that God delights in revealing Himself to His creation then we start to understand why knowing Him is our highest calling.

Coming to know God means that we will understand the character of God – that He is a God of kindness, justice, and righteousness. A God of balance. Not just a God who loves us, but also a God who has certain rules and that there is justice in those rules, which in turn leads to His righteousness.

In our devotional life, when we get to know God and we are able to live in a conscious awareness of His presence, then who and what He is will rub off on us. Then we will become an extension of what we know of Him. The more we seek Him, the more we will find out about Him and His character, then the more we will become like His Son.

Have you ever stopped and considered that in the whole of God's creation, there is only one part of that creation that is not fulfilling naturally what God intended? The earth, the plants, the sky, sun, moon, stars, animal life, everything is doing what it was created for except mankind. God created man to have a relationship with Him and if left to himself Man would never fulfil that desire of God. The moment Adam sinned the whole of mankind was cut off from the presence of God. God sent His Son so that we can once again have that relationship with God and live in His presence. We are falling short of the ultimate desire of God for communion with His creation.

God has provided all that He can. Now the ball is in our court to seek that relationship with God so that we can bring glory to His name. Getting to know God and becoming intimate with Him begins with an appreciation of His love for us expressed in Jesus Christ's death in our place.

Daniel placed upon himself a discipline in order to know God. A part of that discipline was to pray three times a day. We do not read of anyone else in scripture that had this discipline. It was something that Daniel did, not something that everyone did. It was such a discipline in his life that even the threat of death would not sway him from it.

I have met many people who have felt condemned because of someone else's style of devotion to God. They have a friend or know someone who gets up at five every morning in order to pray and study their Bible before their day commences. Others who read a whole chapter, or book of the Bible each day. Then we have those who pray for an hour every day. Those who keep a prayer journal and record every thing God says to them and each answer to prayer. I am not condemning any of these because they are all very good. At some stage of my walk with God I have used all of them. What I want us to look at is the fact that none of these prove that we have a good, live, devotional life. They can all be part of it, but none of them prove it. Whatever discipline we place upon ourselves we stand and fall to God alone. There is nothing right and nothing wrong. We work it out ourselves.

It is interesting when reading in the Acts of the Apostles, that when Paul was reaching out to the Gentiles he never mentioned prayer, Bible study or any other form of discipline (Acts 15:28–29). Have you also ever considered what the Apostles did on the day of Pentecost when three thousand people were added to the church? They could not tell them to go and read their Bible every day. The only scriptures available were in the synagogue, and these were written on large scrolls which were so heavy that it took a fully grown man to carry them. They could hardly carry their Bible to work with them!

Yet so much of our follow-up work of new Christians is to tell them they **must** read their Bible every day. We then need ask ourselves the question about those who cannot read, and those who are blind. What about those who are in countries where they do not have a Bible available to them? My God is greater than being tied up to us reading every day. No, it is relationship in communion with God that will count. Yes, it is good for us to read our Bibles, endeavouring to do it every day, but when we cannot or it does not happen, don't allow anyone to condemn you.

What form our communion with God takes is our own decision. It is important that we have that special time when we communicate with God and He communicates back to us.

Some years ago when we visited Burundi and Rwanda, I decided that each morning while the rest of the team were at breakfast, I was going to spend that hour seeking God. This was a discipline that I set myself for the entire three weeks. I also determined that I was going to ask nothing from God, but worship Him for who He was and listen to Him talking to me. I wrote down those things that I felt He was saying to me. Looking at those notes now it is interesting to see the things which He did speak to me about. It concerned our church, my family, my own life; direction for the future, confirmation that I was doing what He desired me to do, assurance that I was His child, promises for the future for my family. Special things all of which I have hidden in my heart, as I wait for God to bring them to pass.

Whatever discipline we lay upon ourselves we must try and do it with all our heart, and to continue in that way.

I often meet people who have made vows to God that they have not fulfilled, especially in the realm of devotions and prayer life. People often stand in meetings and commit themselves to pray or to spend a certain time in prayer, and they fail to keep that vow. I know that God will forgive us, but God also says quite a lot about keeping our words and the vows we make (Numbers 6; Numbers 30:2–5; Deuteronomy 23:21–22; Ecclesiastes 5:4–6).

Whatever we feel is right for our devotional life we need to be fully committed to. Whatever you choose to do, do not copy someone else. Do your own thing, work out your own style. We can take examples from others, but it needs to be done in life and not duty. We must not let the example of others condemn us.

There are many people who find themselves living for the Lord out of duty and not out of devotion. Believing that if they do right, they will be right. The Bible makes it clear that it is not what we do that counts with God but what we are that is important.

Romans 8:1–2 and Galatians 5:1 both clearly tell us that Christ has given us freedom, so don't allow anyone to put you under any bondage. Paul uses the word 'yoke'. A yoke is put upon you. It typifies slavery, servitude, bondage, weight. Usually it will mean that someone is training you. The most common use is that of a farmer ploughing a field. I have seen this many times when I have been abroad but it is not usual in our country. A farmer needs to train a young animal to pull a plough. He takes a yoke, puts his old animal in one side of the yoke and the new young animal in the other side. The two animals are yoked together in such a way that whatever the older animal does the younger one will automatically do. It is impossible for the young animal to do anything else but follow the actions of the older animal. Paul was saying that people will try and place this kind of yoke upon us in order to make us conform to their ways. He goes on to say that we have to stand firm in the liberty which Christ has given us. Sometimes the yoke can be hard to bear because it is made of rough wood and it chafes on the back of the neck. Jesus told us in Matthew 11:29–30 that when we take His yoke upon ourselves it will be easy. To be yoked to Jesus is the right kind of yoke for us to bear for He will only lead us in the right paths for us, but to be yoked to another person in order to conform to them is wrong. When we are truly yoked to Jesus then it will be an easy thing for us to become like Him.

Chapter 7

Becoming a Worshipper

The Bible has numerous accounts of people who worshipped the Lord for assorted reasons, in differing ways, and at varying times. Included in our devotional life should be true worship of the Lord. In Matthew 26:7–13 we have the incident where a woman came to Jesus with an alabaster jar of very expensive perfume. We are led to understand that the value of this perfume would have been about a whole year's wages. She poured this upon Jesus' head as He was reclining at table. When the disciples saw this they were indignant and asked Jesus why He allowed such waste. They said that the perfume could have been sold for a very good price and the money given away to the poor. After all, those were the very people who Jesus had come to help. I am sure if we were there when this happened we would have had the same sort of reaction. Jesus' reply would have caused us just as much indignation. He reply was to ask why they were harassing the woman. What she had done was a beautiful thing. He told them that they would always have the poor with them but He would not always be there. What she was doing was in preparation for His burial. Wherever the gospel would be preached throughout the world, what she had done would also be told, in memory of her. We are not told the woman's name, just that it was a woman who came and anointed the feet of Jesus with her perfume. Please take note that Jesus did not rebuke her but accepted her act, because He knew that she was doing it out of an act of worship to her God.

In Acts 16:14 we are told of Lydia, a worshipper of God. This lady opened her heart and responded to Paul's message. She was a dealer in purple cloth from the city of Thyatira. This probably meant that she was a business woman, for in Bible days purple cloth was only worn by the very rich and famous. It was expensive to make. The purple dye to make the cloth came from the sea urchin, therefore she would have needed divers to obtain them. In all we could say she was a prosperous lady but she was still a worshipper of God. It does not matter if we are poor or rich, we still need to be a worshipper.

In Exodus 15:20–21 we read when the children of Israel had been led out of Egypt by Moses, they had seen the Egyptians drowned in the Red Sea. Miriam leads the women in worship to God. Each of us should have the element of an outward expression of worship in our devotion to God.

In Luke 1:46–55 we have the worship of Mary to God when she visited Elizabeth and heard about John the Baptist's conception. This is a true example of what worship should be, a spontaneous outburst of praise from a heart that is overflowing with thanks to God.

It is also interesting to see from the Bible that it was not always Christians, or godly people who are reported to have worshipped. In Luke 8:26–38 and Mark 5:6–20 we have the story of 'Legion', who was possessed by demons. Some translations report that he fell at Jesus' feet and worshipped Him. His worship came before he had been delivered of the demons! I believe this points to the fact that it is not necessary to attain some special plain of spirituality before we worship. Worship should be an expression of our heart to God, and acknowledgement of God's greatness.

There are many definitions for worship, none which fully expresses what the Bible means by worship. Worship will always require an act of our will. We decide to worship. We don't need a special time or place to worship. Like our devotion to God, we can do it at any time in any place, however we wish to. We decide when we want to worship.

Jesus told the Samaritan women in John 4:23 that a time is coming and has now come, when the true worshippers will worship the Father in spirit and truth, for they are the kind of worshippers the Father seeks. Notice in your Bible that the word 'spirit' has a small 's' indicating that it is our spirit that we worship God with, not the Holy Spirit. Although for those who are filled with the Holy Spirit there will be times when we also worship God with and in the Holy Spirit.

One of the sacrifices that the children of Israel were told to offer in the Old Testament was a peace offering. This offering was to be offered when there was no other offering they could make. It was a spontaneous offering just because they desired to bring some sacrifice and worship God. In the Psalms and also in Jeremiah it is called the sacrifice of Praise. An offering up to God of praise in worship to Him for no other reason but that they loved Him.

Just as I believe a devotional life is a life style, so I also believe that worship is a life style. I believe both will run concurrently, side by side integrated into each other – devotion and worship. Devotion being the attitude of our heart and worship being the outcome of that heart attitude.

Chapter 8

Having Things in Their Right Place

One morning some time ago, I woke with a vivid series of pictures. It was the time in the waking process when one is not fully awake yet not asleep. It is often at these times that I know God speaks very directly and clearly to me. I also find that the pictures which leave a lasting impression on me are those that I am familiar with and have a real life application. So it was that morning.

People who know me well know that I enjoy wild life, and am renowned for feeding the birds that come into our garden. These particular pictures used just this interest to arouse me.

It started with me coming out of my bedroom and being confronted with birds flying around. They were beautiful wild birds, and one in particular took my attention. It was a British jay. For those of you not familiar with our British birds, the jay is one of our more colourful ones. I quickly opened a window and after a considerable time got rid of this bird and the others automatically followed it. I then 'saw' myself walking down our stairs. As I came to the bottom step I was alarmed to find that in the hall and kitchen were wild animals. Rabbits, squirrels, foxes, mice, etc. I eventually put them all outside; some were easy and others more difficult to extract. When they had all gone I had to clear up the mess that they had made. I can remember being surprised there was so little;

51

somehow with them departing there seemed to be very little to do. By this time I was more awake and started to ask the Lord what this all meant. As I am not the sort of person who has dreams, if I am woken by something like this I look to Him for what He wanted to say to me.

This is what I felt He was communicating to me. Each of these birds and animals were beautiful. They were created by Him, and that they were for our pleasure and enjoyment but, yes the proverbial **but**, they were in the wrong place! They were not meant to live in homes. 'OK Lord,' I said, 'I can take that but what are you trying to tell me?' There are things in our lives that are all very legitimate, they are things that God has made for us to enjoy but they are in the wrong place. They are taking up positions in our life that God did not intend them to take. They can be family, friends, possessions, a home, a car, children, or a child, a career, a job, or anything else. God wants us to have and enjoy all these things, but when they are in the wrong place they will cause us great concern, and play havoc with our lives. Some of these things will be easy to extract. Others will be more difficult and take a little more time. Some of the smaller things may take longer to remove. Some will automatically follow others when put in their right place. If you allow the importance of this to impress you and you then apply it to your own lives, I believe God will also speak to you.

Later on that day while still thinking about what God had shown me, I felt that He also impressed upon me that some of these things were what we would call 'spiritual' things.

Constantly reading our Bibles without becoming a doer of what we read. Church attendance. Spiritual gifts. Ministry. An excessive concern for our pastor, home-group leader, or prayer partner. All of these are very legitimate things for us as Christians but none of them should take a wrong place in our lives.

It is so easy for us to allow other things to take the place of God. In the Old Testament we have the story of the time when the Lord judged Israel and sent snakes among them to bite them (Numbers 21). It tells us how God delivered His people from the effect of the snake bites. God told Moses to make a bronze snake and put it up on a pole. Then when anyone was bitten by a snake and looked at the bronze snake, he would live and not die. (This was a picture of Jesus being raised on the cross and saving those who look to Him from the effect of Satan's [the serpent] power in their life.) Further on we read that the children of Israel turned this bronze snake into a thing to be worshipped (2 Kings 18:42). Hezekiah broke the bronze snake in pieces for the Israelites had been burning incense to it (2 Kings 18:42). They had taken the very thing that God had used to deliver them, and worshipped it instead of God. (Today there are some Christians who appear to worship the cross more than the Saviour.)

One example from the Word of God is the life of King Solomon (1 Kings 11:1–6). Solomon was told by God that he was not to marry any foreign wives. Yet we understand from the Bible that Solomon disobeyed God and married foreign women. As a result they turned his heart away from God and he was not fully devoted to the Lord his God, as David his father had been. We can easily be drawn away from being fully devoted to the Lord by the things we allow ourselves to love. It was legitimate for Solomon to have wives, but it was not legitimate for him to have foreign wives. Now obviously there was a time when he only had one foreign wife, but by allowing that one into his life he had opened the way for more. God had repeated His command to Solomon personally at the dedication of the Temple that he built (1 Kings 9:1–9). Although God spoke to Solomon personally he did not repent. He carried on with his own way of life.

Following this example through and then applying it to ourselves, we see how often we 'get away' with one act of disobedience but that one act often leads to another and then another. This happens when there has been no true repentance. When there is no true repentance our hearts are quickly turned away from being fully devoted to God. Solomon was the wisest man who has ever lived, so we are told. His heart must have been right in its devotion to begin with because he requested God to give him a heart of wisdom so he could lead God's people righteously. One act of disobedience without true repentance, led him to an end out of God's will. Because when God spoke to Solomon he hardened his heart to God's voice and commandments, and as a result he lost God's favour. Let this be a lesson to us today. An example is something we learn by. Many modern Christians have not learnt the lessons which the Old Testament has taught us. They have said that in God's New Covenant it is all grace and liberty, and they have forgotten what God has said.

When you meet God and hear His voice, do not harden your heart as Solomon did. Solomon still lived with the wisdom God gave him but he had no more revelations from God, and no more direct communication with Him.

Personal ambition is another of the things that often hinders us from truly seeking the Lord and being wholly devoted to Him. In Psalm 24:3 the question is asked – *'Who may ascend the hill of the Lord?'* Today we have many people who climb rock faces or mountains just for the sheer fun of it. It is something that gets their adrenalin running and once they have conquered one there is always another to challenge them. We also see people climb the hill of a career, or strive to reach a particular goal in life. We don't find many people climbing the hill of the Lord in order to stand in His holy place.

I can remember when the world's highest mountain was climbed for the very first time. I was nine years old, and as a special treat we were taken by our school to the local cinema to see the newscast of Edmund Hillary and Tensing Norgay's climb of Everest. For weeks Hillary and Norgay had been climbing treacherous terrain in order to conqueror Everest, then on the 29th May 1953 at approximately 11.45 am they reached the summit. Years of preparation had gone into it, and thousands of pounds

54

sterling. But what did they accomplish? Just fifteen minutes standing on top of the world! Because of the conditions they had to quickly descend. Fifteen minutes, that was all.

The difference for us is that when we climb the hill of the Lord and stand upon His holy hill the conditions are such that we can live there for the rest of our lives. We never need to descend! One thing is certain; it will cost us a lot, both in time, commitment, and energy. Another thing that is also certain is that we will be in the place where God dwells. We can live in His presence continually once we have conquered the difficult terrain at the base of the mountain. What is that terrain? What does it consist of? What will it mean to us to attain this mountain peak?

- It will mean saying no to self-ambition.
- We will have to cross the valley of man-pleasing.
- Find our way through the dense forest of Satan's deception and lies.
- Fight the chill of separation from the world.
- Battle with the wild animals of our own thoughts.

Then we will be able to stand upon His holy hill and do what Psalm 99:9 tells us:

> *'Exalt the LORD our God and worship at his holy mountain, for the LORD our God is holy.'*

So the challenge remains for us to ask ourselves these questions:

- Which mountain are we trying to climb, the hill of the Lord or the hill of self-ambition?
- Are we climbing the wrong mountain?
- Is self-ambition stopping us from the number one priority in our life: that of seeking God?

Chapter 9

Lordship

Earlier I mentioned that there is a danger of becoming so familiar with the things of God that we miss recognising His voice when He desires to communicate with us. There is also a danger that we become so familiar with the words that we use as a Christian, that we miss the full impact of them. Words like – King, Lord, Saviour and Christ. Yes, they are all names used for Jesus, but do we fully understand them? What is a King? What is a Lord? What is a Saviour? What is meant by Christ?

I hope that all of us who have been born-again know the reality of Jesus Christ as our Saviour. He is the one who paid the ransom for us, the one who rescued us from sin, the one who laid down His life for us. We can relate to this aspect of the Lord Jesus Christ. Because it is tangible, we can grasp the true meaning of Saviour.

The title 'Christ', means 'the anointed one', the Messiah. He is the one who has authority. It denotes His relationship to God, it describes a relationship of equality. This was the very thing which the Jews understood and for which they took up stones to stone Him in John 10:30–33, when He claimed to be one with His Father. It emphasizes His role as the revealer of God the Father, for it is through His role as Christ that we can come to know God.

Probably most of us, at least those who come from the churches which are known as 'charismatic', 'pentecostal', or the 'new' churches have heard sermons, or read articles and books about the Kingdom of God. Therefore we have an understanding of Jesus being King. This speaks to us of government. The final authority, the one who has laid out the laws which govern the Kingdom. Those of us who live in a Kingdom here on this earth have a little understanding of this type of government.

Now we come to this word 'Lord'. It is one that we find quite often in the scriptures. In the New International Version of the Bible it is used 7484 times. I would conclude therefore that it is quite important to God and then to us in our relationship to Him. We know that the word Lord is used in both the Old and New Testaments, both of God and of Jesus. In the book of Revelation it is used of both (Revelation 19:6; Revelation 22:20). We sing it so many times and use it in prayer a vast amount, but what do we understand and mean when we use it?

Paul tells us in Romans 10:9 that if we confess with our mouth that 'Jesus is Lord' and believe in our heart that God raised Him from the dead then we will be saved. How many times we have sung and declared the Lordship of Christ, no one will ever know or count. I feel there is a difference in declaring the Lordship of Christ in spiritual warfare and confessing that Jesus Christ is **my** Lord. There is something very personal required when with our own mouth we confess that Jesus is our Lord. In Colossians 2:6 Paul tells us that, just as you received Christ Jesus as Lord, we must continue to live in Him. It would appear to me that there is something very real about the Lordship of Christ in our lives. If, and when, the gospel of the Lord Jesus Christ is preached in its fullness there will be this dimension of Lordship also proclaimed. It is my experience that quite a number of people are born again without a true knowledge of the Lordship of Christ. I know that there will be many who say that it is impossible to be born again without making Jesus Lord. That is a theological point that I do not wish to go into. The gospel is both simple to receive and understand. Jesus brought salvation into the realm of the understanding of the 'common' people. We do not need any depth of theology to understand that we can be saved from our sin and become a new creation. We also do not need any depth of intelligence to understand Lordship. But we do need a surrender of our will to the Lordship of Christ.

You already know how I started my walk with God, and most likely there are many of you reading this who can identify with me. Coming through 'the church' as I did, I had no real understanding of confessing the Lordship of Christ. For me it so happened that the reality of Jesus Christ being my Lord came after my initial commitment. There was a period when I went through a process of surrendering my whole life to the Lordship of Christ.

I believe this concept is seen in Exodus chapter 21, where instruction is given to the children of Israel concerning their slaves. In verses 5 and 6 we read:

> *'But if the servant declares, "I love my master and my wife and children and do not want to go free," then his master must take him before the judges. He shall take him to the door or the doorpost and pierce his ear with an awl. Then he will be his servant for life.'*

It is not so many years ago that a very popular chorus had the line in it, 'Pierce my ear, oh Lord!' It was taken from this passage, conveying the meaning that we have surrendered our life to the Lordship of Jesus Christ and we would be His slave for life.

I can hear many people shouting at me – 'but I am a son of God not a slave.' Yes, I agree 100 hundred percent with you. In relationship to God I am a son, but in my attitude to God I have made myself as a slave to Him.

Peter tells us in 1 Peter 3:15 *'But in your hearts set apart Christ as Lord.'* There is then an actual act of setting Christ as the Lord of our life. It requires an act of our will, when we surrender our whole life over to the Lordship of Jesus Christ.

In Revelation 19:16 we see the statement:

'KING OF KINGS AND LORD OF LORDS.'

I believe there is a difference between the Lordship of Jesus Christ in our lives and His Kingship. When I surrendered to His Lordship I made myself a servant of Jesus Christ. When I became born-again then I was made a citizen of His Kingdom. As a citizen I am obedient to the laws of the kingdom, as a servant to my Lord I serve Him in whatever area He requires me to work in. Two different relationships.

I have mentioned the fact that we surrender our whole life over to His Lordship, but in reality, the way it works out is on a daily basis. I need to surrender my will to His whenever there is an issue involved that demands a giving up of my will. Because yesterday I said 'no' to self and 'yes' to Him does not mean that it will be the same today! I will daily have the challenge of His Lordship in my life. There was a time in my life when I, like the slave to the Hebrew master, said to the Lord, I do not wish to go free. I desire to serve you all my life. This did not mean that forever after it would be an automatic act of my will. God has given me a free will and I can either follow my commitment that I made years ago and remain in my Master's service, or as an act of my will I can refuse to surrender on a particular issue. If I do the latter it will have consequences in my life, but it does not take away from the fact that I still have my free will.

Surrender to the Lordship of Christ is an on-going act of my will. It is also a relationship which I develop within my devotional life with God. We cannot go very far into a relationship with God without meeting the challenge of His Lordship.

The Lordship of Jesus Christ in our lives runs parallel to our previous thoughts of things that take the wrong place in our lives. We can only have one Lord in our life, in the same way as we can only have one God in our life. That they are the same makes no difference to the reality of our surrendering to His Lordship, and the actual worship and adoration of our God.

Chapter 10

Priorities

Our priority is our relationship with God. He should be number one, and nothing should come before Him. When we have 'things' which are in the wrong place in our lives then we will not have God in this number one position.

Priorities are things we often hear spoken about, but many of us find difficult to maintain consistently. Because our circumstances change we think our priorities change.

When God created the universe He had priorities, and order in those priorities. Earth came before creatures, plants and food came before animals. We read this is Mark 4:27–29. The planting of seeds comes before growth and the reaping. It is impossible to reap if there has been no planting.

Whatever we try to do, whether it is to bake a cake or make a dress, there has to be an order of priorities to follow if we want it to be a success. Matthew 6:33 tells us to seek **first**, before anything else, the Kingdom of God and His righteousness. The importance is to seek God; not an experience, not a manifestation of God's power, nor a demonstration of God's ability. Seek God for who He is, just for Himself. The scriptures are clear that when we seek Him we will find Him (Proverbs 8:17). They are also clear about a number of other things concerning our seeking God.

- That we need to seek God with all our heart (Deuteronomy 4:29).
- That there is nothing we will lack if we seek Him (Psalm 34:10).
- That we must seek Him while He can be found (Isaiah 55:6).
- That we will be rewarded when we seek Him earnestly (Hebrews 11:6).

When we truly seek God, we will meet God. That is God's promise to us, so there is no doubt about it. God does not hide Himself away somewhere where we cannot find Him. Scripture makes this clear, but there are a few conditions. Deuteronomy 4:29 gives us the condition on how to seek the Lord. It is with **all** your heart and with **all** your soul. In other words, our entire being will be seeking God; not just our spirits. The whole of our being will be desirous of Him. We have a promise from God Himself that when we seek Him we will find Him (Proverbs 8:17).

One important aspect in seeking God is our faith. If we do not have a positive faith towards God, we will not please Him and will also receive nothing from Him.

> *'And without faith it is impossible to please God . . . and He rewards those who earnestly seek him.'*
>
> (Hebrews 11:6)

When we have an encounter with God there will always be something we can tangibly talk about, for when we meet Him He will always do something in our life. We cannot meet with God and not be changed in some way.

Seek means to search out, to pursue, to diligently go after. Not just to look at, nor to casually look for, but to go after with all your energy. You will spend every spare moment available to you going after God.

In recent years I have been concerned about the casualness of many Christians. There appears to be no vitality about their seeking God.

We need to create the determination that we are going to meet with God if it is the last thing we ever do in this life.

Then we need to ask ourselves a question: have I become so pre-occupied with my survival that God would need to do something dramatic to attract my attention? Perhaps a prophecy, miracle, or other manifestation. Our walk with God should be an on-going relationship so that we can hear God's voice without a burning bush.

When we have made our relationship with God our number one priority in life, our devotional life will become as natural to us as breathing. It will become such a part of us, it will not be a struggle each day to find time to communion with God, no matter what we are involved in.

Chapter 11

Calling and Ministry

As I said in my introduction, I am not entering into any controversy over whether a woman should be allowed to minister etc. What I do desire is to give some help to those women who feel that they have something from God to give.

The specific call that I felt God gave me – the ministry of helps – is quite ambiguous. A help can be anything yet everything, in any way, and in any area. I have always been willing for God to use me at any time and in any way. Don and I can still clearly remember the time before we were married, when we knelt together at an altar rail. This happened after seeing a missionary film. We said 'Lord, you can take us at any time to any place, together or apart. We are giving ourselves to You for You to use!' Because of this commitment I have never felt that anything God required of me would be outside of His will for me as a woman. To make yourself available to God is the key issue. Like Jesus's own mother Mary, when the angel came to her and her response was one of willingness and availability for God to use her. She was not perturbed about the consequences of having a child out of wedlock. She was just submitting to God's will. This has been my own attitude throughout the last 35 years. 'I am willing Lord, for whatever you want. If that means that you require me to do something which is not usually acceptable to people, then the prerogative is yours and not mine!' There have also been the times when what is required of me has not been the thing that I would have wished or desired; times when it meant a sacrifice for me; times when what was required of me was a hardship; times when I have felt isolated and on my own. But when God called, I answered 'yes' to that call. I surrendered to the will of God. There were no promises that it was going to be easy, no commitment that it was all going to be a bed of roses. Incidentally, have you ever considered that in a bed of roses there are numerous thorns? After all, the gifts and calls and ministries are all God's, and through the Holy Spirit He can distribute them all just as He desires, upon whom He desires, whenever He desires.

One day while reading my Bible I discovered this wonderful verse in Job 23:13. Job is talking about God and he says:

> *'But he stands alone, and who can oppose him? He does whatever he pleases.'*

It is totally God's responsibility to use whatever is available to Him.

The Old Testament records that once the only thing available to Him to speak to His prophet who was going a little wayward, was a donkey, so God used it! (Numbers 22:28). The key is availability to God.

Another point I would like to make, is that whatever way God uses us will always come out of our relationship with Him. There are a couple of things the Bible shows us are vitally important to anyone who wants God to use them.

The first is that we do not have to push our own gift. In Proverbs 18:16 there is a general statement made about a gift:

> *'A gift opens the way for the giver and ushers him into the presence of the great.'*

I apply this verse to any gift, no matter if it is a natural gift, a material gift, a ministry gift, or any other gift, it applies to them all. If God has given you a gift then when you use that gift, it will naturally make a way for you before all men. We so often think that we must push ourselves to use what God has given us. I believe this is the main reason why many women have ended up being criticised. In some cases they have even been thrown out of churches, or at least written off by some as being unscriptural! If you have a gift, then just be natural about it and allow God to find the room for that gift.

The other point, is that when a farmer sows his seed he is the first one to receive the fruit of his labour (2 Timothy 2:6). We will be the first ones to reap the seed we sow. We will be the first to benefit from whatever seeds we sow in our relationship with God. Whatever revelation God gives us from His word, we need to be the first one to partake, then we can give it away to others. From the abundance that God gives us we have something to give away. If we are not sowing good seeds in our relationship with God, then we will not reap good fruit in our life. We certainly will have nothing to give away to others. For you can only give what you have received. Paul said:

> *'For I received from the Lord what I also passed on to you: . . .'* (1 Corinthians 11:23)

Paul said that he was passing on what he had directly received from the Lord. He was not there when the last supper took place (which is the context that he is speaking in), but Paul had received directly from God Himself. He was now imparting to his hearers what he had received by revelation. This is exactly what we must do. Pass on to faithful men the things which we have been taught by God. The things which God reveals to us in our own walk and relationship with Him. When this happens there is a certain vibrancy about the message, for we will be able to impart life and not the dead letter of what we have just read or heard from someone else.

A good illustration from our life-style here in the western world is to look at a postman. Someone writes you a letter and it is delivered to your door by the postman. He does not knock on the door, wait for you to read the letter and then make sure you carry out any instructions in the letter. No, he delivers the letter to your door and then he leaves the responsibility with you. There are many people today who, when carrying a message for God to His people, want to check up that the person has carried out all that God has said. That responsibility is for the person who receives the message. In the Bible we have the story of Jonah, who had a message from God for the people of Nineveh. He delivered the message and then went outside the city, sat down, and waited for God to do what he had conveyed in the message. What happened? The city repented and nothing of what God said might happen, happened. As a result Jonah got angry with God. It is not our job to carry out the message we give. It is up to God to bring about the fulfilment of His word. All we have to do is to be a willing handmaiden, making ourselves available for God to use.

I feel that there is a difference between a gift that God gives us to use in His Church in order to bring glory to His name, and the gift of salvation that He has given to us through the cross of Jesus Christ. Salvation touches our 'inner man'. It grows just as a seed grows and brings fruit to our spiritual life. A 'gift' will affect the outer woman, more than our inner life. There is a vast difference between the outward clothing and the inward filling of the Holy Spirit's work. The Holy Spirit's power anoints us with a gift that touches the outward. The Holy Spirit infills our inner life and touches our heart and spirit. The anointing given with the gift does not necessarily touch the heart. It will not change our character unless we allow it to. The infilling of the Spirit deals with heart issues. What our world, and churches need, are people who have been transformed by the inner working of the Holy Spirit. Not just gifted people who are outwardly empowered with oratory and professionalism. We have seen far too many 'stuntmen', and 'superstars', who can produce a wonderful performance. What God is calling for I believe, are people who are transformed by the power of the Holy Spirit. This is what the message of the gospel is – transformation of ordinary people.

I believe that God calls people to all kinds of work, not just to full-time Christian work. We need teachers, nurses, doctors, bank clerks, business managers, factory workers, and all other kinds of workers, to be called by God.

There are people I have met who feel that God would never call them to a particular job because they would enjoy doing it too much. There is the feeling that God only calls people to jobs they would not enjoy doing. God wants us to enjoy our work and particularly any work that He has called and ordained us to do. God wants us to enjoy **all** that we do.

Chapter 12

Time

Many of you may be wondering what time has got to do with your relationship and devotional life? Time is probably one of the, if not **the**, major enemies of our devotional life. Time is also the excuse so many of us use for not seeking God.

An aspect of time that we so easily forget, is that time is created. God created time, day and night, seed-time and harvest, summer and winter. We have time, and to say we don't is often a cover-up for not wanting to find time.

Jesus said that He had completed the work His Father had given Him to do (John 17:4).

This was not the same as saying He had finished everything He could possibly think of to do, nor that He had done everything others wanted Him to do. He made no claims to have done what He wanted, only to do have done what God His Father had given Him to do. This is an important clue for us – God's work is appointed work, there is always time to do the will of God.

The problem with so many of us is that we get frustrated because we feel that we do not have time. There will always be time to do what God wants us to do. Worry or frustration is not in the will of God for His children. The Bible tells us not to worry and be anxious, because God cares for us (Philippians 4:6; 1 Peter 5:7). We so easily have our hearts diverted from totally seeking after God.

Perhaps, because of the privilege of visiting many different countries and experiencing different values and life styles, I have been struck by the wide gap between cultures, particularly in the different values placed upon time. One thing that has stood out for me is the western world's rat race. The pace of life is so fast, whereas in the less developed countries that I have visited, life just 'happens'. There is time for everything, and no one is in a hurry to do anything. This became very real to me during one of our visits to Chile. We had been invited to call on one of the local mayors. During the conversation with him he asked me what was one of the most evident contrasts between his country and mine. At that time, one of the things that really frustrated me was their time-keeping. If we were told that we had an appointment at 10 o'clock, we would all be ready by five minutes to ten. Invariably we would not be picked up until 10.30. For us in our western culture this was unspeakable. So I commented on this. His reply not only helped me to understand the reasoning behind their approach, but also made me re-think my priorities. I was told that in Chile friendship is far more important than anything else. Therefore, if while going to work, or going to an appointment you met a friend, you would not just greet them, but more than likely you would go and have coffee with them! Time was not as important as friendship! I am sure there are many of us who could learn much from this.

Ecclesiastes 3:7 tells us that there is a time to be silent and a time to speak. There is a time to be quiet and contemplative, and this leads me into the next subject – quietness.

Chapter 13

Quietness

One issue I am constantly challenged with, is that of quietness. I should think all women have been challenged by the verse in 1 Peter 3:4 that tells us our beauty should be that of our inner self, the unfading beauty of a gentle and quiet spirit. We are also told that this is of great worth in God's sight. Often when reading this I have had a desire in my heart to attain this gentle and quiet spirit. It is something I do not possess. Those who know me will affirm this, but nevertheless it is something I still wish to progress towards. One day I felt the Lord show me something new about this verse.

I saw that it is of great worth to God, therefore it is right that I should desire it. God made me with my personality and that I cannot change. My character however, how I behave, my actions, my thoughts, my attitudes, how I conduct myself, are things that I can change. I talk more about character in Part Two.

What is meant by a quiet spirit?

Spirit is our inner being; it is something that comes from within. In order to develop this quiet spirit I saw that I needed to spend time on my own developing a peace and a calm within myself. This meant that it would come out of my trust and what I know of God. Isaiah 32:17 tells us that the righteousness we receive when we are a child of God will result in quietness and confidence. Also in Isaiah

30:15 we are told that in quietness and trust we will find our strength.

Quietness begins by trying to spend some time each day on your own. It does not mean that you have to do something special, like praying, reading your Bible or some other spiritual book. Just to be on your own so you can still your heart and mind before God. Start by spending time each day alone. Take time to listen to your own heart and spirit. This is where and when we will learn to worship God for Himself. This is in addition to your devotional time with God. Learning to set your minds on things above will begin with a conscious willingness to think about 'things above', God, righteousness, etc. This should be a time when we do not think about preparing food, shopping, washing, ironing, our job, letters, filing, patients, clients, etc. No, it is a time when we train ourselves to listen to our hearts and our spirit; our inner selves, and God.

If we desire to know when God wants to use us, or when He wants to direct us in a specific way, then first of all we need to listen to our spirits, in a time of quietness. Then we will be able to recognise the way God communicates to us. Then when we are in meetings, we will know when God is speaking to us, wanting us to share something with the whole assembly. If we do not teach ourselves to learn, we will never know when His Spirit is speaking to us. Many people are so hooked on noise that they cannot break the habit. They constantly have to have the radio or tape on, or CD playing, or they are always singing or whistling or making some kind of noise. There are some people who believe that quietness is a type of insanity!

One important element involved with quietness is rest. We cannot expect to be quiet in our inner selves if we have not yet found our rest in God. Throughout scriptures there is the principle of rest. In the Old Testament we find that God in giving His laws to the children of Israel gave very strict instructions about rest. There were days of rest for every person and animal. Years when the land had to lay at rest. Times when it is said of God that He gave His people rest from wars. Rest it would appear, is important to God. It is even said that God rested after He had created the universe. It is a good Bible study to do on our own, so that we can fully realise what God meant by **His rest** (Exodus 33:14; Psalm 62:5; Psalm 91:1; Isaiah 30:15; Isaiah 32:18; Matthew 11:28; Matthew 11:29; Hebrews 4:1–11). Rest is something which all of us require at times. But the rest that we need to find is in God and can only be found in our relationship with Him. It is a relaxation, a respite. It means to unwind. A place where there is no battle, the war is over, we have ceased to fight God and we have harmony with Him.

In music a 'rest' is a time when there is nothing happening, there are no instruments playing. This is a good illustration of what rest should be in our lives. To have a place in our lives where the fighting has ceased. Where there is no noise. Nothing taking place that will hinder our spirits from having that place with God so that we can know true peace and harmony with His Spirit.

I remember a few years ago, when reading my Bible I felt God direct me to verse 11 in 1 Thessalonians 4, where it tells us to:

> 'Make it your ambition to lead a quiet life, to mind your own business and to work with your hands . . . '

I did not fully grasp what God was saying to me at first. A quiet life: that was surely a joke. How could I, a wife and mother, working in an office, travelling with my husband, taking seminars at camps and conferences, running a very busy home, visiting ageing parents, being an active member of a vibrant church, coping with children's activities and school functions, live a quiet life? Ha! Ha! I thought, God you are joking, and laughing at me! Inside I had a little giggle with God, for I could only consider that a quiet life meant inactivity. About six months later I again felt God directing me to this verse. 'Lord, we have been through all this once and you know it is an impossibility for me, so forget it!' I felt very strongly that God was wanting to say something else to me about it so I meditated upon the verse for a few days longer. Then one day 'Eureka!' I had it. What God was trying to communicate with me was the fact that this was a life-style concept, a tranquillity of spirit, peace. Not rushing around, no panic stations, no getting flustered, but a peaceful existence. After all, God was still on the throne. He had total control of the world and my life, so why should I be constantly living at breakneck speed? I began to understand what God was trying to get through to me. I also began to understand in a new way what God's rest should mean in our lives.

Another aspect of quietness and rest is waiting. Many times in the Psalms David expresses that he is waiting upon God (Psalm 5:3; Psalm 27:14; Psalm 33:20; Psalm 119:166; Psalm 130:5). In Psalm 37:7 he gives us the instruction to be still before the LORD and wait patiently for Him. So often we rush through our prayer time expecting God to be in just as big a hurry as we are. Then there are the times when He wishes us to wait upon Him. Another way of putting it is that we are to stay, or remain, in His presence, anticipating His move. In the royal family there were, at one time, people who held the title 'lady-in-waiting', a person who waited upon the Queen ready to meet her every need. In the same way I believe we should be waiting upon God, only moving when He has given us something to do. Jesus told us that He only did the things that His father showed Him and taught Him (John 5:19–20; John 8:28; John 12:49–50; John 15:15). When we have taught ourselves the art of quietness, having entered into the rest that is ours, then we will be able to wait upon God to know what He would have us do.

Chapter 14

Pressure

Pressure is a subject that we consistently hear being spoken about in counselling and Christian conversation. People make statements like:
- 'I've got too much pressure on me at the moment!'
- 'I cannot cope, the pressure is too great!'
- 'That's the straw that broke the camel's back!'

In these kinds of situations the thing that usually gets pushed out is the one thing that should help us cope with the pressure. That is our communion with God.

When the pressure is on for our time, more often than not it is the 'unseen' that goes first. We cut short our time spent with God and before long it is non-existent.

> *'We do not want you to be uninformed, brothers, about the hardships we suffered in the province of Asia. We were under great pressure, far beyond our ability to endure, so that we despaired even of life.'*
>
> (2 Corinthians 1:8)

It would appear from this that Paul also had great pressure placed upon him. So much so that he despaired for his life. Does this sound familiar to you? Have you been in the place that you have felt like giving up, committing suicide even?

Pressure will challenge us to compromise, perhaps even

to get angry. Paul's expression of despairing even of life is a human reaction, in just the same way as we may react in anger.

Paul goes on to explain why the pressure came:

> *'Indeed, in our hearts we felt the sentence of death. But this happened that we might not rely on ourselves but on God, who raises the dead.'*   (2 Corinthians 1:9)

The pressure was there in order that he would not rely upon himself, but that he would put his whole trust and reliance upon God. One of the major purposes of pressure is so that we may learn to depend upon God and not upon ourselves.

Paul then continues:

> *'He has delivered us from such a deadly peril, and he will deliver us. On him we have set our hope that he will continue to deliver us.'*   (2 Corinthians 1:10)

It is interesting that Paul makes three statements here which reveals where he placed his trust:
- **He has delivered us,**
- **He will deliver us,**
- **He will continue to deliver us.**

If we have known God's deliverance once then we can be sure that He will deliver us again and that He will continue to deliver us. It obviously depends upon where we put our trust. Is it in God or is it in our own ability to cope?

When the pressure is turned on, we must accept the challenge:
- **first** to our number one priority – our communion with God;
- **secondly** to our human reactions; and
- **thirdly** to our trust in God's ability to deliver us.

That will then lead to a **fourth** challenge:
- just how much we really **know** God.

All pressure is not bad – but whatever challenges our walk with God and our human-ness, will always be a good pressure, for it will develop our spirituality and we will find out where we really are with God.

Our devotion to God should be something which we cannot do without, our life depends upon it. Out of our devotion to God will come the strength that we need to face life with all its trials and temptations. It will also assist us in our service for God. Our devotional life should reflect all of this. No matter when or where that nourishment takes place, morning, noon, or night, the important thing is that it does take place.

PART TWO

The Character of a Godly Woman

Chapter 15

To Be Like Jesus

To be like Jesus,
To be like Jesus,
All I ask to be like Him.

These are the words of a chorus that was sung about the time that I came into a real experience with God. I can recall many times singing this very lustily, meaning it with all my heart. I am not sure at the time that I knew what it fully meant. Looking back now, I realise more the significance of those words. The next part of our journey in knowing God comes when we realise that God wants us to live a life that resembles the life of His Son Jesus Christ.

When we begin to look at the life of Jesus with the concept that it is a life that we must emulate, we can easily become despondent and feel that we are never going to be able to attain to that standard. I know I did, and for a period of time I gave up trying. Then one day I began to see that God did not require something from me which He was not also going to assist me in.

There are a number of scriptures that teach us that God has given us the means to be like His Son – Romans 8:29; 1 Corinthians 15:49; 2 Corinthians 3:18. I am persuaded that in order for me to become like Jesus, God has not left me to myself. He has provided all that I need to become like His Son. God's goal for my life is perfection, not that

I will reach that goal here on this earth, but I can begin the process (Matthew 5:48; Philippians 3:12–14; Colossians 1:28).

I am also convinced that God wants me to do all I can towards that goal. God has done all that He can do in giving us His Son. Jesus died in our place in order that we can receive God's power. It is this power, the power of God, that will assist us in reaching His goal for us. The goal He desires us to reach is to be like His Son, Jesus Christ. I have had many women talk to me about their personal struggles in trying to reach this goal. In the light of this I want to share with you the things which God took me through in coming to the place I am in today.

Chapter 16

Who Am I?

Who am I? It is a question that many of us ask when we are seeking an identity. In order to answer the question we must start with who God has made us.

We need to come before God as women who He has created in His own image, and made to hold a part of Himself. We are a vital part of His creation, people who will bring glory to His name. In Genesis 1:26–27 God said,

> *'Let us make man in our own image, in the image of God he created him; male and female.'*

Women were not an after-thought on God's part, we were in God's heart from the very beginning. We were not made because Adam needed a partner. Yes, woman was made to complete man, but I don't believe that was the only reason why God made us. God made male and female in the order He did, in the way He did, so man could not be independent.

Eve was created equal with Adam in relationship to God. Eve was created in God's image just as much as Adam was. She was an intricate part of God's plan. She had a very special role to play in God's whole creation. A part of God's character was placed within Eve. This was very different from Adam's character but it was still a part of God. Eve was made with all the capabilities to be who and what God had in mind for her. She was not wanting in any area.

The life which Adam and Eve lost because of sin has been restored to us through the resurrection of Jesus Christ. Today I believe we can live the life God intended us to live from the beginning of time. I believe that God created us as women to have a special expression of His likeness in us. This is unique to us as women and not at all like a masculine expression of God. I am fully convinced that as a woman I am created as much in God's likeness as man is. Because I am of a feminine gender does not mean that I do not possess a part of God's character.

I therefore believe that there are certain character virtues which we as women must seek to build into our lives. These are things that we should possess because we are feminine. There are also character virtues that we should have in our lives that should be in every child of God no matter whether male or female. This is really what this section is all about. The character of a child of God, with a special emphasis for us as women.

Character is something that we do not hear so much about in our churches. It would appear that there is the feeling that it is enough to become a child of God, then everything else will automatically follow. I have also heard an idea expressed that implies that it does not matter what our character is like, the only really important thing is that we have a gift or a calling from God. This gives the impression that God will overlook our character traits, even those that are ungodly. If we have a gift or calling from God then our character must be right. In my experience I have realised this is often not the reality we see in many people who profess to be called of God. For many years my husband and I have been seeking to build character into those we are responsible for before God. I feel that many of the tragedies that the church of God has experienced over the past decade of ministers who have fallen, have often come about because a gift, or calling, or ministry as taken prominence over character. It has been said many times that 'character precedes function'. In other words we should be more concerned about the character of a person than the person's gift.

It has always been of interest to me that in the early church when the Apostles needed someone to do the mundane task of administrating the daily portions to the widows in the temple, we are told that they chose seven men who were **full** of the Holy Spirit and wisdom (Acts 6:2–7). These men were noticed for their character. Stephen is mentioned in particular as being full of faith. Today when there is a job in our churches to be done, it is often the person chosen who has the most time, or the most talent, but in fact I believe it should be the person who has the right character of God in their life. Whether that be a woman or a man does not matter, the thing that should be noticed is the character of the person.

Character is something that we all have, yes, but we do not all possess the character of Christ. The Bible is written in order for us to reach that goal.

One of the mistakes that has befallen us women has been the desire to minister without the character to carry that ministry. Therefore throughout the history of the church we have had women who have been easily led, who have ended up bringing disrepute on the church because they have omitted to look to their character before they launched into a ministry they felt God had called them to. They have mistakenly believed that once God has gifted you there must be an immediate response to exercise that gift. We miss the point which scripture teaches us. Many of the heroes of the Bible had long periods of training before they manifested their ministry.

Abraham received his 'word from God' when he was 75 years old, but it was not totally fulfilled until he was 120 years old. A difference of 45 years. For many of us we would feel this was a life-time! David was anointed king as a young man but it was many years before he actually became king. We are told by historians and theologians that from the time Paul received the Damascus Road experience until he started his apostolic ministry there seems to be a period of about 19 years! Many of us believe that as soon as Paul had received his sight, after the encounter with God, he commenced his ministry. Not so. God had a time of preparation for him to pass through.

As women in God's church I believe we have to live down many of the misconceptions and mistakes of the past. I put it this way. There are remarks made on numerous occasions about 'women drivers'. Whenever anything goes wrong on the road you will often hear the statement made 'oh, I expect it was a woman driver!' I happen to be a woman who drives many miles every year. I am known to be quite an efficient driver, very capable of coping with most types of roads and road conditions. To accomplish this I have had to live through and disprove the philosophy that says all women drivers are bad and incompetent.

In the same way, I believe that women in the church must live through (that means coming out the other end), and prove to be women who can handle the Word of God efficiently, honourably, and with maturity and understanding. In order to do this we need to lay down many of the attitudes that have been put into us by the world but also by many so-called 'Christian' people.

We must seek to develop our character. Even when we feel and know with certainty that God has called us and given us a gift. We must not plunge ahead, walking over God's anointed men, but we must submit our life to God and allow Him to manifest what He has placed within us. After all, the ministry and gifts are His not ours. We do not have to protect His gifts.

So the answer to the question 'Who am I?', is that each one of us is a child of God, created in His likeness in order to have a relationship with Him, made with the ability to be like Jesus. Because we are made in His likeness we can develop His character within us. Each of us have gifts that He has created within and we must discover what these gifts are so that we can bring glory to Him.

Chapter 17

Character

I can remember as a teenager that I often heard people say – 'You get like those you live with!' Meaning that whoever you spend the majority of your time with, in the end you will pick up their ways and their character traits. Although not a direct quotation from the Bible I believe we see the principle there in scripture (1 Corinthians 15:33).

If this applies to bad company it must also apply to good company! If we spend our time with godly, good people, we will pick up good character traits. Surely then if we spend time with God, and develop a consciousness of the presence of God, we will develop godly character traits.

The main passage of scripture which gives us an insight into some of the characteristics of a Christian is 2 Peter 1:3–9. Let us look at this scripture right from the first verse in detail. Our attention is drawn first of all to the fact that it is **His divine power** that has given us **everything** we need to live a godly life.

Note it is **His** power, not our strength or ability. There is nothing that we have done that has given us what we need to live by. God has done it. He gave us our human body, He has also given us the ability to have a relationship with Himself. It is His divine power that has done this. No human has been able, or will ever be able, to create life. They can only make good imitations, whether it is a silk or plastic flower, or a machine that works like a human brain (the computer), they are all only imitations of the real thing. God's power is the beginning of all meaningful life.

This comes through our **knowledge of Him**. That knowledge has come to us because of **His glory and goodness**. Although God has made all this available to us it is then up to us to receive all these things, and we can only do that through coming to know God Himself.

It is because of this glory and goodness that **we have been given great and precious promises**. Many years ago there was a saying around that as Christians we should be 'standing on the promises, not sitting in the premises!' There are Christians who are still only sitting in the premises, i.e. a church building, or perhaps sitting with people who are a church, but they themselves have never made the promises of God their possession. If we are going to be effective in our walk with God the promises of God must become reality in our lives and be more than just print on paper that we read on occasions.

We may be partakers of His divine nature by entering into the promises that He has given to us, and thereby escape the **corruption of the world** in which we live and all its evil desires, which were brought upon mankind by Adam and Eve's sin. The reason God has made all this available to us is so that we can have a quality of life that reflects His divine nature.

Because of this, **we must make every effort to add** certain things to our lives. God has then left the ball firmly in our court. We have to do all we can to become partakers of His divine nature. There is something that we have to do and that is to add these characteristics to our life.

Faith; knowledge; self-control; perseverance; godliness; brotherly kindness; love. For this reason we are told that we need to have these qualities in our life is so that we will not be **ineffective** and **unproductive** in our walk with God. If we do not make an effort to develop these qualities in our life then we are told that we are **near-sighted**. This means we can only see our own needs. We are **blind**, that means we see nothing around us. Worse than this we have **forgotten that we have been cleansed** from our own sin, and forgiven.

I wish to spend a little while looking very briefly at these virtues, and also fruits of the Holy Spirit, which we find in Galatians 5:22–23. I hope to whet your appetite so that you will look further into them for yourself and begin to work them into your life. Underlying all I have to say, please bear in mind that it is God's promise that He will help us in all of these things. His desire is that we are effective and productive in our walk with Him. He has not given us a relationship with Him just so that we can be happy in ourselves, but that we will be effective in our relationships down here on this earth, reproducing it in others. That is what is meant by discipleship.

Paul while writing to the Romans, tells us that if we are going to have characters that will reflect the glory of God then there is one thing for certain. We should rejoice when we go through any form of trial or suffering because it is only as we go through these that our characters are going to be refined (Romans 5:3–4).

It is my desire for us to look into the characters that are listed in the two passages we have quoted from 2 Peter and Galatians. Added to those I have four other characteristics that I feel are of vital importance to us, although they are in scripture they are not listed in the above two passages.

Chapter 20

Faith

Faith is a much preached about subject. A subject which I feel some have become over-balanced on. Don't turn off before I begin. Faith is a very practical thing that each of us need in our lives. It is not just something for preachers with signs and wonders ministries. According to the Word of God it is that which God's people should live by (Habakkuk 2:4).

In Hebrews 11 two women are listed as heroes of faith – Rahab, even though she was not even a child of Israel, and Sarah. We know that when Sarah heard the man of God telling her husband what was about to happen to them, she laughed (Genesis 18:12). So we could not consider then that she had faith. In some aspect we could even say that she was doubtful. What qualified Sarah to be listed with all these heroes of faith? I believe it was the fact that when she saw the Word of God being fulfilled in her life she started to act in faith (Genesis 21:7). The Word of God also tells us as women that we will be daughters of Sarah if we do what is right and do not give way to fear (1 Peter 3:6). To be called a daughter of someone means that we have something of their make-up in us. One of the characteristics which will be recognisable in us as being daughters of Sarah will be our faith. The opposite to faith is fear. If Sarah had given way to fear she would never have borne Abraham his promised son. Just think for a

90

moment; once Sarah realised that she was pregnant, especially at her age, she could well have thought about all the negatives. She could have been thinking within herself that she would not be able to carry a baby that long and probably considering that her body was not strong enough to give birth. Looking into the future a little, she could also have been wondering if she would be able to feed the baby. Because of her age all the physical functions involved in giving birth would have ceased. It would appear that Sarah did not look at these things. I believe that at the moment she realised she was pregnant, her faith rose. She began to realise that what the angel had said was actually going to happen. Fear would have stopped her, but instead her faith carried her through a situation which seems totally impossible to our human minds. This is the kind of faith that we need. A faith which will carry us through all the things we find in our lives that look like impossible situations.

Many of us today only see faith in the realm of mighty miracles. I believe some of the big international 'ministries' that focus on signs and wonders, have done a disservice to the body of Christ. It would appear that they have taught Christians that the only reason we need faith today is to produce miraculous signs of God's power. In truth, the Bible teaches us that every child of God should have faith. Jesus himself told his disciples in Mark 11:22 that they should *'have faith in God.'* They were not to marvel over the withering of the fig tree for they were going to see greater things than this. It was more important for them to have faith in God than to have faith in mighty signs. We also see that Jesus told His disciples to rejoice that their names were written in the Book of Life more than rejoicing that demons were subject to them! (Luke 10:17–20).

It is more important for us to have faith in God and to receive power from Him to live by than it is to receive power to cast out devils!

On another occasion Jesus asked his disciples *'Where is*

your faith?' (Luke 8:25). I would like to ask you the same question – 'Where is **your** faith?' Is it in God or is it in demonstrations of the power of God? I believe it is very important that our faith is directed in the right way and for the right reasons. Not so that people can pat us on the back and tell us how good we have been. Nor that we receive the acclaim of man because signs and wonders happen when we pray. I believe that there has been a misconception about the ministry involving signs and wonders. Many seem to think that because signs and wonders follow their ministry then that is God's stamp of approval upon their life. It would appear that this has given them a licence to live how they like, without a real conviction of sin, having no sense of right or wrong. Some of them have no real relationships of any value. There is no one who can speak into their lives when they need help. But my Bible tells me that I need faith to live righteously (Romans 1:17). This kind of faith comes through one thing and that is the Word of God. It does not come because we pray much, or because of the number of times we go to meetings. It does not come because we read our Bible every day. Nor yet because our church is the best church around. It comes through hearing the message of the Word of God. What is that message? The whole of the message of the Bible is that we can have a right relationship with God as our Father. Romans 10:17 instructs us that faith comes from hearing the message, and the message is heard through the Word of Christ. Jesus Himself told us that the scriptures teach that:

> *'Man does not live on bread alone, but on every word that comes from the mouth of God.'* (Matthew 4:4)

It is only in the Word of God that we will find the nourishment that our faith needs in order to grow. God has given faith to each one of us (Romans 12:3). By this I mean that every human being has the capacity to believe God and have faith. Some use it and by using it they develop their faith, others don't use what they have and never develop a faith that works for them. One Gospel singer put it this way – 'Faith is spelt R-I-S-K!' If we do not reach out we will never begin to use our faith and we will never know what our faith can bring us from God. We must start by risking. In other words, putting ourselves out on a limb, to a place where we have to trust and rely upon God because there is nothing else for us to do. We must only do this when we know that we are moving in a realm where we have a promise of God's provision. Because I know a call from God to the ministry of helps, I can move in faith in any area that I know is within that call and be sure that God will be there. I am moving within the faith I have an assurance about, because I have God's call.

1 Corinthians 2:5 tells us that our faith should be in God's power and not on anything of man's wisdom. Then in 2 Corinthians 5:7 Paul tells us that we live by faith, not by sight. We live by what we know in our heart about God, not on what our eyes tell us. It is interesting that Paul considers our faith is something that can grow and develop (2 Corinthians 10:15). The more we know of God, the greater our faith will become. That is the way our faith grows. Our very relationship with God can only work as we put our faith in Jesus Christ (Galatians 3:26).

It is only as we have faith in Jesus Christ that we can approach God and begin our relationship with Him (Ephesians 3:12). A few verses on in Ephesians 3:17, we see that it is only by our faith that Christ will dwell in our hearts.

We then come to the amazing statement in Hebrews 11:6, where we are told that if we are going to please God it must start with us having faith in who God is and in the fact that He exists. We are then told in 1 John 5:4 that if we are going to live in victory we will only be able to do it by our own faith.

If we are ever going to accomplish anything in our walk with God it will only be by faith. No matter how hard we work at our Christian experience, how many good deeds we do, or how much we wear ourselves out working for God, all of it will be of no benefit if we do not do it all by and through faith.

To help us understand this subject a little I want us to look at an incident from the life of Jesus. In Matthew 15:22–28 we are told that a Canaanite woman came to Him, crying out for mercy because her daughter was suffering terribly from demon possession. Jesus did not answer a word, so His disciples urged Him to send her away. Jesus replied that He was sent only to the lost sheep of Israel. The woman came and knelt before Him and cried out again for help. He replied that it was not right to take the children's bread and give it to the dogs. She replied that even the dogs eat the crumbs that fall from their masters' table. Jesus told her that she had great faith and that her request was granted. Her daughter was healed.

This dear mother had put herself out on a limb, she had come to Jesus for her child. Jesus' reply to her request was one that she could easily have taken exception to and gone away discouraged and rejected. As if that were not enough when she asked for His help, His reply was to call her a dog! Still she was not put off, she acknowledged her position and then asked for some crumbs. In other words, 'Lord I only want a little and I believe you will give it me.' As a result of her persistence her daughter was healed. She came knowing that she was an outcast and not acceptable, she got called a dog, yet still her faith would not let her give up. She put herself in a very vulnerable position; everything was against her but her faith refused to take no for an answer. We need to start like Sarah and believe that God will do what He says He will do. Then take the example of this mother and press through with our faith. We can have a faith which will not only receive from God what we need but also be able to help others, just as this mother did for her daughter.

Chapter 19

Knowledge

No matter where we look in this world we will find people thirsting for knowledge. Whatever area of life we come from or are in at this present time, knowledge is important to us. The Bible tells us that:

> *'Of making of many books there is no end, and much study wearies the body.'* (Ecclesiastes 12:12)

There are whole buildings full of books and computers that store incredible amounts of knowledge. All of this knowledge is of no eternal value to us if we do not have the first ingredient in our lives – a knowledge of God. What we know of God, His workings and His Word, is the knowledge that we need to live an effective Christian life.

Experience is something that no one can teach you, you have to acquire it on your own. The Psalmist (Psalm 119:66) prays to God that He would teach him knowledge and good judgment, for he believed God's commands.

Knowledge means that we have an understanding of a subject, not a casual cursory knowing, but deep perception. We will only get this through our relationship with God.

We are told in Proverbs 1:7 that the fear of the LORD is the beginning of knowledge. Later on we will be looking into the fear of the Lord, but for now I want us to consider that the fear of the Lord is only the beginning of knowledge. It is where we start to accumulate our knowledge. We read this again in Proverbs 9:10. In this verse, added to the fear of the Lord being the beginning of wisdom, is the statement that knowledge of the Holy One is understanding. This give us the thought that once we know God, we will then have understanding.

Knowledge is often coupled in the Word of God with our knowing God. Knowing God will obviously therefore develop our knowledge, not only of God Himself but also of all the other things which He requires us to know about (2 Corinthians 2:14; 2 Corinthians 4:6).

Paul, it would appear, is expecting us to develop this knowledge until we become proficient with it. We see this in 2 Corinthians 8:7 where he tells us that we should excel in everything; *'in faith, in speech, in knowledge.'* Then in Ephesians 4:13 we are told that God has given gifts and ministries to the Church:

> *'until we all reach unity in the faith and in the knowledge of the Son of God and become mature, attaining to the whole measure of the fullness of Christ.'*

If we are ever going to become the church that God desires, then we are going to have to somehow receive the knowledge which Paul so earnestly desires us to have. He equates this knowledge with our becoming mature, growing in our walk with God and our knowledge of Him (Colossians 1:10).

Doing a word study from the Bible it is interesting to discover how many subjects the scriptures refer to as things which we should have knowledge about. I have listed just a few below.

- knowledge about the secrets of the kingdom of heaven (Matthew 13:11).
- knowledge of salvation (Luke 1:77).
- knowledge of God (Romans 1:28).

- knowledge of the glory of God (2 Corinthians 4:6).
- knowledge of the Son of God (Ephesians 4:13).
- knowledge so that you may be able to discern (Philippians 1:9).
- knowledge of His will (Colossians 1:9).
- knowledge of the truth (1 Timothy 2:4).

If we begin to increase our knowledge of the above subjects then we will at least make a start in developing this character in our lives.

Our knowledge will only develop as we put ourselves in a position to acquire knowledge. When we look at our natural life we commence our education (in Britain) around the age of five. We then have eleven years of formal education. Some people also go on to further education and specialise in various areas of trade, commerce, or another profession. All to acquire knowledge. Most people still confess that when they have reached middle-age they are still learning. The Bible says that there are some who are always learning but never able to acknowledge the truth (2 Timothy 3:7). The truth is only to be found in Jesus. Jesus told us Himself that He was the way, the truth and the life (John 14:6). We will always be in the process of learning. As those who are the children of God we have the advantage that we will come to know truth because we know the One who is Truth.

Just as we place ourselves in schools and colleges to acquire earthly knowledge, so we need to place ourselves in the position to acquire heavenly – spiritual – knowledge. We do this by reading the Word of God, and having a relationship with God, in order that we can be led into all truth by His Spirit.

So we see that because we are children of God, we cannot opt out of acquiring knowledge. What needs to change now that we are children of God, are the subjects we acquire knowledge about. Our priority should be knowledge about the things of God.

Chapter 20

Self-Control

This is a subject that we hear just a little about but which never seems to come to fullness in our lives.

Proverbs 25:28 says that a man who lacks self-control is like a city whose walls are broken down. I believe that this means that if we do not develop self-control then we are vulnerable to attack from our enemy. When our defences are down it is easy for him to enter and play havoc with our lives. Not every enemy who enters a city is there to destroy it openly. Some enemies are there as spies in order to search out any weakness. Others are there to undermine the governmental authority and to cause anarchy. This is also how Satan subtly moves into our lives.

Self-control is in reality just that, self under control. But under whose or what control is the ultimate question.

In Galatians 5:22–23 we have the list of the fruits of the Holy Spirit, one of which is self-control. It is clear to me that this means that self must be under the control of the Holy Spirit. For one of the fruits of the Spirit working in our lives will be self under control.

Self out of control is what we term as lust; not a word commonly in use today but still a word that is used often in scripture. For further study look at Romans 1:27; Ephesians 4:19; Colossians 3:5; 1 Thessalonians 4:5; 1 Peter 4:3; 1 John 2:16.

Lust means appetite, desire, greed, passion, to covet, to

crave. It means an uncontrollable desire for anything, whether it is good or evil. We must never allow our emotions to run riot. Self must always be controlled.

One area in which I needed this virtue to work in my life was in the realm of the emotion of anger. I was born with a very quick temper, and over the years it had become a real weakness in my life. One day after I had been filled with the Holy Spirit, while reading Galatians 5:22–24 the word self-control really struck me. I began to feel that God was wanting to deal with me in the whole area of my temper and having it under control. I began to see that it was one of the fruits of the Holy Spirit. If I was really filled with the Holy Spirit, one of the evidences would be that the fruits of the Spirit were evident in my life. How much I needed the fruit of self-control became clear to me. I prayed and started to believe God that He would help me in this area. I can remember very vividly the times when I had thrown things at my brother in sheer anger. Controlling that anger was not easy. It was something that I had to work at. It took time, but thankfully I can now look back and see that as I grew in my relationship with God, allowing His Spirit to flow through me, self-control has been seen in my life. I do not live in cloud cuckoo-land. I still have the emotion of anger within me. Since I am still living in this human body, I have the ability of anger within my emotions, but I also have the Holy Spirit, and the fruit of His presence will be anger under control.

The Bible tells us in Ephesians 4:26:

> *' "In your anger do not sin": Do not let the sun go down while you are still angry.'*

Anger in itself is not sin, it is an emotion, but how we handle it and what we do with our anger will determine if we sin or not. It is like being tempted. Temptation is not sin. It is one of the tools of Satan to try and trick us. If it were sin then Jesus would have sinned, because He was tempted in all points as we are, yet He did not sin (Hebrews 2:18; Hebrews 4:15; James 1:14). What we do when we are tempted determines if we sin or not. To yield to the temptation is sin. In the same way, to yield to the emotion of anger may cause us to sin. But when we feel angry, if we yield to the Holy Spirit we will know the fruit of self-control in our lives, and we will not sin in our anger.

Chapter 21

Perseverance

When considering perseverance one of the main Bible characters to look at is Job:

> '...you have heard of Job's perseverance and have seen what the Lord finally brought about.'
>
> (James 5:11)

The word perseverance is not commonly in use today, either as a word or as a virtue. So what do we mean when we use the word?

Perseverance means to have endurance, longsuffering, persistence, and steadfastness. In today's society this is something that we seem to have given up on. If something doesn't happen in the way we want it to we give up on it.

It was not so long ago that I can remember a message being brought to the church by many itinerant preachers, about being a finisher and not just a starter. The principle of seeing an issue through and not giving up until it is finished, is a principle that we definitely see in scripture. In the same way, God is not going to give up on us. The parable of the prodigal son is our main example. But what about us? Do we have this same principle or do we quickly relinquish our goals?

One of the lessons that the scripture teaches us is that when we go through any trial or temptation, the thing that will be produced in our life is perseverance (Romans 5:3–5; 2 Thessalonians 1:4; James 1:3–4).

If it is our desire to reach maturity, and I trust that for most of us this is our goal, the above scripture references will teach us that the testing of our faith and the perseverance that it will produce will help towards making us that mature and complete Christian. God also desires us to come to maturity. There are many more scriptures which we can study which will help us: 2 Timothy 2:12; Romans 15:5; Colossians 1:11–12; 1 Timothy 6:11; Revelation 14:12.

The thought of rejoicing when suffering and trials come, is one that is foreign to our human minds. One of our problems is that we do not seem to **know** that when we are tested in the area of faith, it will bring about perseverance as the verse in James says.

It is like the illustration often quoted of the lady who came for prayer. When the minister asked her what she needed prayer for her reply came that she needed more patience. The minister promptly prayed, 'Lord, please give my sister more tribulation!' The lady quickly retaliated saying, 'It's not tribulation I need prayer for, it is patience!' Back came the reply, 'But, Sister, the Bible tells us that tribulation works patience!' (Colossians 1:10–12; Colossians 3:12).

If we are going to persevere with anything we are also going to need the virtue of patience in our lives. So often in scripture perseverance and endurance are coupled with patience. Patience is a virtue that we hear spoken of quite often. We hear people say that someone has 'the patience of Job'.

Unless we are tested we will never know if we have patience and perseverance. For someone to profess to be patient means that they have had the circumstance in which to test if they have the virtue.

The question we often hear asked is – 'Why me Lord?' Especially when we feel that we have circumstances and situations in our life which we are unable to view positively. We seem to be able only to see them negatively. We shout at God 'Why me Lord?' 'Why did this have to come just now?' 'Why is it always me that seems to get the short straw?''Why has God allowed this to come into my life?' We seem to forget many of the principles of the Word of God.

A reason why God permits us to go through some of the things that we wish we did not have to go through, is in order to develop our character.

Notice in the verses we looked at in Romans, Paul starts with the suffering, and continues with perseverance, which in turn gives us hope.

When circumstances in our life appear which we dislike, or wish had not come, what is our reaction to them? Do we face them as Paul says with rejoicing? Or do we react to them negatively?

Cast your mind back to the story of Job. Satan came before God in order to test Job. He was convinced that he could get him to deny God. What was the result? God knew that Job would not give in. He knew that Job's character was strong enough to take what Satan could bring against him, so God allowed Satan to do all he could. Please note that Satan could only go as far as God allowed him, also that Satan had to ask for permission to afflict Job. The Bible tells us that Satan said to God that there was a hedge about Job (Job 1:10–11). We can conclude from this that God had His own protection around Job. God had to allow the hedge to be penetrated before Satan could enter. This was before the Cross and Resurrection of Jesus Christ. This was before the outpouring of the Holy Spirit. Why do we think that things have changed for God's people today, and that God has let down his fences around us?

Job's character possessed a confidence in his God that is lacking in many of us today. Job said:

> *'But He knows the way that I take; when He has tested me, I will come forth as gold.'*   (Job 23:10)

Job knew that he could trust God to bring him through. He also knew that the only thing that could happen to him was that he would be better at the end of it. The end of the story of Job is that he has twice as much as he had at the beginning (Job 34 :10). Both spiritually and materially Job was a better man. Oh, if only we could possess this quality today: that whatever came our way we could see it as developing our character. Considering it as something which God has allowed in order that we will be more like His Son after the experience.

There have been many times, especially in the early days of my walk with God that I have been tempted to ask 'Why me Lord?' Times when I have felt the burden was too heavy. Occasions when I wished that He had not chosen me. I have found that the longer I have known God, the times that I think this way has become less. This is because the more I get to know God, the more I realise that He will not let anything come my way which He will not also equip me to bear.

One such time was at the birth of our seventh grandson, which is our ninth grandchild! He came two weeks early which is not unusual, especially for a first baby. Our son Joel and his wife Julie were not quite ready. They thought they had another two weeks, but God likes to give us surprises. So on the 22nd December 1995 Benjamin decided it was time to grace us with his presence.

I am so glad that God knows far in advance all that will happen to us. Having a family of five children, Christmas is always a busy time. It is also a time when we usually have extra people stay in our home. Most Christmases we would have up to twelve for the period leading up to Christmas and over the New Year. This Christmas was to be different. Our last child, our daughter Faith, had been married in the previous May. My husband and I thought that we would have the type of Christmas that I often had thought I would like. A nice quiet time with very few folk around. This year looked as though it was going to be ideal. The last of our family had 'flown the nest' and so it was decided quite early that we would have just Joel and Julie around on Christmas day. As they were expecting their first child it would mean that Julie would not have too much of a burden in the last few weeks of her pregnancy. It was going to be a relaxed day. Don's mother would be with us as usual for Christmas lunch and part of the afternoon, but apart from that there would be no one else. Little did we know what was in store.

The first thing happened in the last week of November. Don's mum had to come and live with us. This was going to mean a time of adjustment both for her and us. Being just a few weeks before Christmas you can imagine what it would have been like if we had planned our usual Christmas.

Benjamin then arrived on the 22nd. By Christmas morning it was discovered that something was drastically wrong. He was unable to digest his feed. He was vomiting, and had various other symptoms, the reasons for which the hospital where he was were not able to be diagnose. So it was decided on Christmas day at about 10 am that he was to be taken to Bristol, a three- to four-hour journey by road. Actually he was flown by Air Ambulance and underwent a major operation at 7.30 pm on Christmas day. During the operation it was found that his upper bowel was not connected to his lower bowel. Later we were told that he was flown by Air Ambulance because he was not expected to live. The surgeon who operated, told us that if he had been left another half an hour he would not have lived! We had not just 24 hours, but a number of days when the situation was uncertain.

God in His wisdom knew what was going to happen, and it was His mercy that we had no one else staying and the day was quiet. There are many more incidents, too numerous to record here, of how we saw God's hand at work in the first week of Benjamin's life.

I tell you this story because it was a time when we had an incredible underlying trust and faith in God that to this day we feel was supernatural. Often we would look at each other and ask 'How do people without God cope with this type of situation?' The peace we knew could only have come from God. The certainty we had, that Benjamin was going to be with us was inexplicable. Looking at our own son and daughter-in-law we saw the presence of God manifested in such a way that we also couldn't explain.

Throughout the whole time I cannot remember once saying to God 'Why us Lord?' My faith in God has come to the place that I knew that Benjamin was going to pull through. Looking back now on the experience, I can detect that there was an underlying knowledge that God had allowed this to happen. God had given us a trial, and it was something that would test our trust in Him. He knew what we could cope with, and He knew that at this time we were in the place to have our faith tested.

Even after Benjamin came home, the first few days were traumatic for all of us. We knew God's sustaining power. I believe that all of us would now say we would have had it no other way. I can see how the whole situation brought us – at least myself – to the place to realise just what God has done in our lives. In the area of trust and faith in God I feel that nothing will come my way unless God also gives all that I will need to take me through it. At the time of this ordeal, whatever the outcome may have been, I knew God was with us and that He would not leave us.

Mrs Rose Kennedy, the mother of J.F. Kennedy, the one-time President of the USA, made this statement – 'God does not give us a cross any heavier than we can bear.' I believe this is borne out by scripture (1 Corinthians 10:13).

It has been said that:

> 'Difficulty is not outside of God's design for our lives, but God is never outside the difficulty, unless we put Him there.'

Perseverance through trials will produce in us character that then gives us a trust in God which also leads to hope.

106

Hope is defined in the dictionary as reliance, trust, aspiration, expectation, anticipation. The opposite to hope is despair, and doubt.

When we look into the scriptures on the subject, we soon find that hope is a well-documented subject. We are told in Psalm 25:3 that no one who puts their hope in God will ever be put to shame. Again in Psalm 25 this time in verse 21, the Psalmist claims that because his hope is in God integrity and uprightness will protect him. Then in Psalm 119:114 the writer says that God is his refuge and shield, and that he has put his hope in God's Word. Proverbs 13:12 tells us that hope deferred makes the heart sick, but a longing fulfilled is a tree of life. It is interesting that the well-known verse 31 in Isaiah 40, is hardly ever quoted correctly! It is those whose hope is in God that will have their strength renewed and mount up as eagles, run and not grow weary, walk and not faint! So often it is translated with the emphasis on those that wait upon the Lord, as though there is something special about the long waiting period, when in fact it is those whose faith is in God for the future, who will be blessed in this way.

In Romans 8:24–25 hope and patience are linked together. Hope is in the future, not in the present. We often say that when we are planning to do something in the future that 'we hope' to do so and so. Paul writing in 2 Corinthians 1:10 says that because of the times that God has delivered us in the past we can now set our hope in the future that He will continue to deliver us.

In Hebrews Paul give us this statement:

> *'We have this hope as an anchor for the soul, firm and secure. It enters the inner sanctuary behind the curtain.'* (Hebrews 6:19)

Hope is the very thing that gets us anchored safely into God. It is not casual, there is a certainty about hope (Hebrews 6:19). We have to hold unswervingly to the hope we profess, because He who promised is faithful

(Hebrews 10:23). The very famous 'faith' chapter of Hebrews 11 starts with this amazing line:

> *'Now faith is being sure of what we hope for and certain of what we do not see.'*

1 Peter 3:5 infers that because the holy women of the past put their hope in God, they were able to make themselves beautiful. So we see that perseverance as a character in our lives will produce a trust and faith in God for the future that will assist us in becoming holy.

Chapter 22

Godliness

In 1 Timothy 4:8 and 1 Timothy 6:6, godliness is said to have value for all things, and godliness with contentment is great gain.

Godliness. God-like-ness. I want us to consider that godliness is a part of the character of God and something that He urges us to possess. It is very noticeable that godliness has value for all things. There is no part of our life that godliness will not affect. When we have godliness in our life, it will be seen. It will effect the way we live and how we conduct ourselves.

One definition of godliness is to be reverent, and respectful, which means it is an attitude. Another verse from 1 Timothy 2:2 gives us instruction that we live peaceful and quiet lives in all godliness and holiness. There is no really clear definition of what godliness is. Many people seem to think it is the same as holiness but it cannot be when it is mentioned in the same verse as holiness. Godliness therefore must be a mystery as we see it referred to in 1 Timothy 3:16. I believe godliness is a part of the character of God that deals with our attitudes, moods and temperament; in other words our disposition. This aligns very clearly with our definition of being respectful. When we are respectful we will be considerate of each other.

Chapter 23

Kindness

Kindness is expressed by consideration, tenderness, and thoughtfulness. In other words being considerate of the people around us, thinking about them and what they need more than thinking about ourselves all the time. Considering how we can make our fellow Christian's life more pleasant, fulfilling their needs.

From the scriptures one of the evidences that we have the Holy Spirit working in our lives, is that there is fruit growing and one of those fruits is kindness (Galatians 5:22–23).

We see from Romans 12:10 that another way of expressing kindness is by loving each other, and honouring one another above ourselves. There are many books written and even more sermons given on the subject of loving our brothers and sisters in Christ (John 13:34; John 13:35; John 15:12; John 15:13; Romans 13:8; Galatians 5:13; Ephesians 4:2; 1 Thessalonians 4:9).

Jesus himself told us in 1 John 4:20, that if anyone says, ' "I love God," yet hates his brother, he is a liar.' He went on to ask that if anyone does not love his brother, who he can see here on this earth, how can he love God, whom he has not yet seen? It appears that if we cannot get along with our brothers down here on this earth that it is unlikely that we will be able to love in the way that we should. So much of what we know of God is only relevant as we work it out here on this earth with the people who are around us.

John goes even further. He tells us that we have been given this command:

> '*Whoever loves God must also love his brother.*'
>
> (1 John 4:21)

Must is a very strong word, there is no way out. Loving our brother is equated with us loving God. This then brings us to the greatest message of the whole Bible – **love**.

Chapter 24

Love

Let us look first of all at our love for God, because this should be foremost in our life. In Luke 10:27 Jesus told us to love the Lord your God with all that you have, heart, soul, strength and mind, and then to *'Love your neighbour as yourself.'* When we truly love God in this way that love will then effect the love we have for our fellow man.

There are some people who find it difficult to love the people they find themselves in church with on a Sunday morning. We have heard story after story as we travel, of people who cannot get along with their Pastor, church leader, deacon, or other official in the church. The amount of times that we have had to pray with and counsel people who have responded to altar calls, after hearing a message about forgiving or loving other people, is immense. We never cease to be amazed at the number of churches that are being made ineffective in their witness by members who are not right with each other, and who backbite one another.

Realising that God has given us the ability to love should help us to love and show love to all, but especially to those in our close church family. I like the word *'poured'* in Romans 5:5, when is says that God has poured His love into us. It implies that it flows easily, that God gives it freely, there is no stopping it, it comes in a good flow whenever we need it. It comes into our hearts, by the power of the Holy Spirit, and there is nothing that we have to do about it but to stand and receive. We do not have to screw up our faces and twist God's arm to let us have enough love in order to be kind and show love to someone, all we have to do it open our hearts and receive!

I quite often become amazed at some people I have observed in meetings, especially prayer meetings. You look at their faces and you would think that they were in the dentists' surgery. They are so intense. Their faces are screwed up tight. It looks as if they are trying to twist God's arm to answer their prayers. Others sometimes shout so loud, you would think God was either deaf, or miles away. How they can relate this as being at rest in God I will never understand.

Then comes the real test. After we have put ourselves right with our brothers and sisters in the church and we feel good that we have begun to love them, God tells us that this really is nothing. Luke 6:32 and 35 tells us that there is no real credit in loving people who already love us, what we need to do is love our enemies. My husband often puts it this way. If we do what God tells us to do and love our enemies it will soon come about that we will have no enemies. Why? Because we will have 'loved them to death'! Meaning that we have loved them until they are no longer enemies.

When we can love those that hate us we will be getting close to becoming like Jesus and we will at least be called the sons of God.

I want to look a little more deeply into what the quality of our love should be. Romans 12:9 tells us that our *'love must be sincere.'* That word 'sincere' is very well bandied about. Do we truly know what it means? Our English word is made up from two Latin words *'sine'* and *'cera'*. *'Sine'* means without and *'cera'* means wax. So to be 'sincere' literally means to be without wax, which seems unusal given its current usage. Why is that? In the past when a silversmith made an article and it was not truly pure, meaning that there was still some dross in the silver because the purification system was not quite so refined as ours is today, the silversmith would fill in the impure part with wax to over it up. As soon as the article was put under any heat the wax would melt and the imperfection would be discovered. So to be sincere means that there is nothing false about us. There is nothing that is being covered up. We are pure in all our dealings and motivations. There is no hidden agenda.

Apply that to our love and we can begin to see what our love must be like. It must be real, not false, or put on. We all must at some time or another, read or heard of the very famous 'love chapter' of the Bible, 1 Corinthians 13. Let us take just one verse, namely verse 8, which says, *'love never fails.'* No matter what else may fail, when our love is sincere it will never fail. It will be like God's love. It will endure forever. Turn over a few pages in our Bible and we come to 1 Corinthians 16:14 that tells us that we should *'do everything in love.'* Whatever we do, no matter who we are doing it for, we must do it out of true love. And yet again another proof that we have the Spirit of God moving in our lives will be the fruit of love (Galatians 5:22). Then we are told in 1 John 3:18, to let us not love with words or tongue but with actions and in truth. Our love should be able to be seen by our actions. Not only so but 1 John 4:16 tells us:

> *'God is love. Whoever lives in love lives in God, and God in him.'*

One of the ways that we know if we are living in God or not is by our love (1 John 4:18).

True love, God's love, which we have already seen is distributed in our hearts by the Holy Spirit, has no fear in it. Our love will not be perfect while we have fear towards the person we are directing our love to. In particular this means fear towards God. There is a right kind of fear, this we will be looking at further on in the book, but the fear we are concerned about here is to be terrified of someone or something. When we know God as our Heavenly Father we will no longer fear, or be terrified of Him. We will be able to approach Him with confidence, having an assurance in our hearts that He will accept us.

Chapter 25

Life and Joy

Our relationship with God should work on a consistent basis. It should not be akin to a yo-yo, up for a period of time and then down for a while. When we have our devotional and prayer life on an even keel, and even our worship of God has become spontaneous, then I believe we will have started to be a partaker of what God has planned from the beginning for us.

What is it that He had planned? **Life** of course, and a life that has a lot of bounce in its step.

Life is something that we will all say we have just because we have breath and move, but this is not true life for the Christian. We saw earlier that from the moment that Adam sinned he began to die, and that process of death he continued to reproduce in his children. 1 Corinthians 15:22 tells us this – *'for as in Adam all die,'* but it does not stop there. It goes on to say – *'so in Christ all will be made alive.'* The good news of the gospel is that Jesus Christ came to buy back all that Adam lost to mankind because of sin. I hope that all Christians not only realise this but that it has become a part of their faith.

Paul teaches us in Romans 6 that just as Jesus died to sin but was made alive again at His resurrection so we should not count ourselves dead to sin but alive to God in Christ Jesus. He repeats this in Colossians 2:13:

> *'When you were dead in your sins and in the uncircumcision of your sinful nature, God made you alive with Christ. He forgave us all our sins.'*

In 1 Peter 3:18 we read again that Christ died once for all, the righteous for the unrighteous in order to bring us to God. He was put to death in the body but made alive by the Spirit. We no longer live a life that is in the process of death when we become a child of God. The life we now live is an eternal life. Although our body may some day die and decay, we have a life that will continue and it is in this dimension of life that we should now be living.

It is a life that is just that, **life**. Jesus told us in John 10:10 that *'the thief,'* who we know to be Satan, comes only to steal, kill and destroy. He, that is Jesus, came that we might have life, and have it to the full. As some translations put it, abundant life. God's desire is that we should enjoy life while here on this earth, but also enjoy a relationship with Him.

I have observed that for many Christians there is no dimension of enjoying life. They seem to give the impression that they have to endure life. They believe that it is impossible for them to enjoy life because if they did God would not accept them. For some it is a feeling that:
- the more adversity they can encompass,
- the greater amount of suffering they can embrace,
- the larger their difficulty in this life,
- the bigger their burden,
- the more tribulation they can go through,

the better the Christian life they will produce. When in reality the opposite is the truth. One thing I am convinced of is that God desires His children to enjoy themselves.

Don and I have five wonderful children and not once would we ever wish to give them anything but happiness. Matthew 7:11 describes this very plainly. One thing is certain; God has only given us good gifts and the best gift He has given us is His life, through His Son Jesus Christ, and He wants us to enjoy His gift of life.

117

Jesus told us much about the joy that He gives us, yet so many of us seem to refuse to enter into and receive what He has died to provide for us. In John 15:11 Jesus says:

> *'I have told you this so that my joy may be in you and that your joy may be complete.'*

Two things here. The first, that it is His joy that will be in us. The second, that He has given us His joy in order that our joy may be complete. Then in John 16:24 He repeats this same thought:

> *'Ask and you will receive, . . . your joy will be complete.'*

It would appear that Jesus is expecting us to request things from Him so that we can receive things that will give us joy. Then in John 17:13 He goes even further. He says:

> *'I say these things so that you may have the full measure of my joy within you.'*

He is wanting us to have a full measure of joy, not half a measure, or three-quarters but a full measure. This means that we can be full of His joy.

Paul tells us in Ephesians 6:2–3:

> *' "Honour your father and mother" – which is the first commandment with a promise – "that it may go well with you and that you may **enjoy** long life on the earth." '*

One of the first commandments which God gave to the children of Israel was because He desired people to live and enjoy a long life on the earth He made for them.

Paul tells Timothy *'to command.'* Notice the strength of this; command, not tell. It is authoritative.

> *'Command those who are rich in this present world not*
> *to be arrogant nor to put their hope in wealth, which is*
> *so uncertain, but to put their hope in God, who richly*
> *provides us with everything for our **enjoyment**.'*
>
> (1 Timothy 6:17)

God has done all that He can do to provide all that we need to live our life to the full and enjoy it while we do.

One of my most favourite books of the Bible is Ecclesiastes. Some people wonder why, but if you read it with an open heart to God you soon discover the truth of what the author is trying to convey. That our life here on earth is futile without the dimension of God. It conveys the concept that outside of God, life is valueless. That God has given us everything to enjoy (Ecclesiastes 2:24).

So many of us do not find this satisfaction. Instead we are frustrated and we even become bogged down under what we call the 'burden of our work'. We simply do not get satisfaction out of our work, let alone enjoy it! Yet God's Word instructs us that we should find both satisfaction and enjoyment out of work. I believe the main reason why we do not find these two is because we have an attitude that work is an endurance. We are not taught as children to work, and to enjoy work. Work is seen as an unavoidable evil, not something that God has given us to enjoy (Ecclesiastes 8:15).

- 'Joy to go with our work? Work is something I **have** to do in order to live! Work is a chore!'
- 'Work is what I do in order to earn a wage so that I can have food, clothes and a roof over my head! As far as enjoying it is concerned I cannot come to terms with work being a joy.'

These are the usual comments we hear if we start to talk to people about work. When we do find someone who enjoys their work they are called a workaholic.

Ecclesiastes 3:22 asks if there is nothing better for man to do but to enjoy his work? Some will react by saying, 'Well I can think of a lot of things that I would like to do rather than work. I'd rather lie in the sun, go on holiday, look around the shops, spend my money (which you wouldn't have if you didn't work!) play with the children, or go for a walk.'

Ecclesiastes 5:19 tells us that whatever we have, wealth and work are gifts from God and we should be happy with them. Not a gift from God one would say, but what my own hands have brought me. I would like to ask the question, who was it who gave you the ability to work in the first place? Who was it who gave you your life so you can work? Everything we have is a gift from God, so why not your work also? In today's society I think anyone who has a job must see it as a gift from God, for there are so many people so do not have jobs that we must be thankful if we do.

Ecclesiastes 11:8 then tells us that no matter how many years we live we should enjoy them all. It is possible, with God, to enjoy the whole of our life.

Some people tell me that all this is Old Testament teaching, and that we are now living in the New Testament and so are under a different set of rules. Sorry, I disagree – for I read in my Bible that the whole of God's Word is given to us for our instruction:

> '*All Scripture is God-breathed and is useful for teaching, rebuking, correcting and training in righteousness, so that the man of God may be thoroughly equipped for every good work.*' (2 Timothy 3:16–17)

All scripture means just what it says; all is an inclusive word, we cannot have all and there be an exclusion. We are also told that the Old Testament is there for our example (Hebrews 4:11). What is an example for if it is not for us to learn by? The Old Testament is there so that we can learn by the mistakes people made, and so we can learn from the good points. It also teaches us so that we can live a better life.

Romans 14:17 does say that the Kingdom of God is a

matter of righteousness, peace and **joy** in the Holy Spirit. Oh, the righteousness bit is all right, and the peace we can cope with, but **joy** in the **Holy Spirit**! That is what the scripture says the Kingdom of God consists of, yet when we look at the people of the Kingdom I see so little of what is expressed here.

Joy is more than laughter, happiness, mirth, gladness, or glee. Joy is a deep down attitude in the heart.

> '... *for the joy of the* LORD *is your strength.*'
> (Nehemiah 8:10)

> '... *you will fill me with joy in your presence, with eternal pleasures at your right hand.*'   (Psalm 16:11)

> '*Restore to me the joy of your salvation* ... '
> (Psalm 51:12)

> '*With joy you will draw water from the wells of salvation.*'   (Isaiah 12:3)

Joy! Joy! Joy! Yes, they are there in your Bible too.

My computer Bible tells me that in the New International Bible, the word joy or joyful arises 246 times, and the word 'enjoyment' or 'to enjoy' appears another 58 times. That's quite a lot. Therefore we can be sure that it is something that God intends us to know about.

I believe to obtain this joy the first step is to recognise that it is part of our inheritance in Christ. It is all a part of our salvation. It is not an added extra, it is something that comes with the package. Joy is what we receive when we receive Christ. All we have to do is to change our attitude towards the dimension of joy and receive it from God. It is not some new big gift that we can have sometime later when we have earned enough 'Brownie points'. It is part of God's gift of eternal life, so let us begin to walk in it. It is also a part of God's character and should therefore be ours.

Chapter 26

Peace

Peace is a subject that we hear spoken of in many areas of life. News broadcasts often speak about peace; heads of states enter into 'Peace Talks'. Peace in some countries means the civil war has ceased, or there has been a cessation of war between neighbouring nations. Then we often hear people making statements like:

– 'Oh, for peace of mind!'
– 'I'd give anything for a little peace and quiet!'
– 'No one can find peace around here!'
– 'Why can't we have peace in our home?'

I have a suspicion that all of us probably at some stage in our life have uttered this type of statement. There are those who want peace at any cost and will hide things in order to bring peace. Others will go to any lengths to have peace. Divorce and the break-up of relationships occur because people want peace. Mankind was not made to live in constant turmoil and unrest. God created us to live in peace and harmony with ourselves and those around us. Why, even one of the names of His Son, whom He sent to bring us His peace, is 'The Prince of Peace'.

The very first place we need to have peace is in our own hearts and lives. Making our own peace with God is the first step to finding true peace. But more than this, there is a peace that God desires His children to live in. One of the covenants that God made with His children in the Old

Testament was a covenant of Peace (Numbers 25:12; Isaiah 54:10; Ezekiel 34:25; Malachi 2:5).

When we begin to look through our Bible on this subject, we soon discover that peace is a commodity that God desires His people to live with and in. One thing which will come out of our relationship with God is peace. Isaiah 32:17 tells us that the fruit of righteousness will be peace in our lives. When we are in right relationship with God there is the possibility that we can live in peace in every area of our life. Once we have made our peace with God then we will have peace within ourselves, peace with those we live with and peace will be the atmosphere we dwell in.

One of the basic elements of the Kingdom of God is peace (Romans 14:17). Once we live in the Kingdom of God, peace should be evident within us. One of the things that Isaiah 53:5 tells us Jesus did for us on the cross, was to take our punishment to bring us peace. Yet so many Christians do not seem to be able to live in peace.

Satan appears to be able to thwart us in this area of our lives so effectively. We allow him to take our peace away. Whether it is peace with God, or peace with our family. It may even be peace in our church, or the atmosphere of peace in our homes. It would appear that he can so easily take this from us. One of the ways to stop this happening is to see that it is our right as children of God to live in peace. Psalm 29:11 gives us the promise that the Lord blesses His people with peace. So peace is one of the blessings which God brings into our lives. Once we have been justified through faith, we have peace with God through our Lord Jesus Christ (Romans 5:1). It is a fact, peace should be our experience as children of God.

It is not a maybe, or if we do some special pilgrimage we will attain this peace. No, once we have received by faith the justification that is ours, we can and shall live in peace.

Even more startling is the verse in Isaiah 26:3 that tells us that God will keep us in perfect peace when our minds are steadfastly set on trust in God. Notice it uses the adjective 'perfect'. It is not partial, it is complete, total, comprehensive, absolute; in other words there is no flaw in this peace. But our minds will only find this peace when we have a steadfast trust in God, and that can only come from our relationship with Him.

Psalm 119:165 talks about the 'great' peace that we can have when we love His Word and then it goes on to say that nothing can make us stumble. The outcome of having God's peace will be a stability.

Colossians 1:20 is very clear that we receive this peace through the blood of Jesus Christ that was shed upon the cross. It is an important thing to note that it is only through the blood of Jesus Christ that we can have this peace. We need to truly appreciate that what we have from God is through the blood of Jesus Christ. It is not just in the death of Jesus Christ. People can die without shedding any blood. When we study the scriptures on the subject of blood, we soon discover that throughout the canon of scripture there is the theme of blood. Blood was involved in all the main sacrifices that the children of Israel had to offer to God. When God redeemed mankind He used the blood of a lamb with which to do it; the Lamb of God – Jesus Christ (John 1:29; 1 Corinthians 5:7; 1 Peter 1:19; Hebrews 9:14–22). It is through this blood sacrifice that we can obtain peace.

Jesus Himself told us that He would not only leave peace with us but also give us His own peace (John 14:27). Because of the peace that He will give us we can live without fear.

A definition of peace is 'freedom from war', or 'the war is over'. There are three main areas that this peace will apply to our lives. The first we have said is to make our peace with God. This then will result in us having peace within ourselves that will in turn help us to live in peace with all men (Romans 5:1; John 14:27; Romans 12:18; Hebrews 12:14). The peace that we can have is one which the world will not be able to give us no matter how many peace talks we have. True peace can and will only come through Jesus Christ. We are also told in Philippians 4:7 that this peace with God will transcend all understanding, and it will also guard our hearts and minds. Therefore it is something that won't just give us a nice feeling of being at peace with ourselves, God and the world, but will also help us in our walk with God. It is this same peace that will assist us with the battle that many of us constantly fight; that of our thought life.

> '*A heart at peace gives life to the body.*'
>
> (Proverbs 14:30)

Yes, it is possible to have peace that will be active in our bodies. But it is only the peace of God that will bring this about. Peace, true peace will result in a total relaxation in the salvation of God. There are doctors today who will openly say that the answer to many people's sickness is for them to be at peace with themselves.

There are many, many more verses from the Bible that we could look at, but time and space does not permit it here. It would be a good study for you to do on your own.

I am persuaded that peace should be in the character of each child of God. It is part of our inheritance in Christ.

Chapter 27

Goodness

When I started to consider this virtue I did my usual thing. When I am not sure of the full meaning of a word I go to the dictionary. This is what I discovered goodness means in today's vernacular – decency, honesty, morality, excellence, value, worth. My, how we need these in our lives.

Honesty. Talking with many people today it would appear that there is hardly a job that one can have that does not involve dishonesty is some way or another. Credit fraud, embezzlement, tax evasion and other forms of dishonesty are always in the media. I read a very interesting statement once in a report on world trends. It said that in recent years in one particular non-Christian country, whenever government offices had need to recruit new workers they asked for Christians. This was because it was discovered that Christians were the only ones they could trust the do the jobs honestly. This was in a country where it is illegal to be a Christian!

Decency. Something else that we constantly hear in the media. Often it is coupled with **morality**. Christians should be both moral and decent. I hope we all know what immorality is, but I also hope we know what morality is. But what does it mean to be decent? What does it mean to be indecent?

> *'Let us behave decently, as in the daytime, not in orgies and drunkenness, not in sexual immorality and debauchery, not in dissension and jealousy.'*
>
> (Romans 13:13)

The Bible instructs us women to dress modestly, with decency and propriety, not with braided hair or gold or pearls or expensive clothes, but with good deeds, appropriate for women who profess to worship God.

Decency will have a different interpretation in different cultures. While visiting the USA on one occasion I was made aware of how the use of English words can vary. Words which in Britain would be classed as swear words or at the least unsavoury, were being used as everyday expressions by the Christian community. At first I was shocked, then I realised that it did not have the same connotation to them. To me it was indecent, to them it was not. In the same way when visiting some African cultures it is acceptable for women to be topless. For us in the Western world it would be considered indecent for a Christian woman to come to church topless! Why the difference? I do not know, but we have to acknowledge the fact that the difference is there.

The key word here for us to look at is what is 'appropriate'. Whatever our culture we must look at what is considered to be appropriate. For a woman to go on a five-mile hike, up a mountain in evening dress and high-heeled shoes, would be inappropriate. Just as it would be for another women to turn up at Buckingham Palace to be presented to our Queen dressed in bedroom slippers and dressing gown, with her hair in rollers.

It would appear that to be decent means to be godly. Therefore we can conclude that to have the character of goodness in our lives means that we are godly, and this we have already looked at.

Excellence, value and worth. When we have truly become a child of God and are able to relate to Him as our Father then I believe these three virtues should be within our grasp. Everything God has ever done has been done in excellence. We see this when we look at His creation. Since we are made in His image I believe we can also have the virtue of excellence within us. Most things that I attempt to do I aim to do my best, for this is the way I consider I can achieve excellence. I feel that when I try to do my best then I have something which I can offer to God with a clear conscience.

No matter how unworthy I feel, or how little I value myself, of this I am sure, that through Jesus Christ I have been made worthy.

Chapter 28

Faithfulness

Faithfulness means to be loyal to, to be steadfast. In Matthew 25:23 Jesus is giving us the injunction to be faithful with the little things God gives us to do, for then He will be able to give us more. Stewardship of what God has given us is involved in faithfulness. Being faithful in prayer is probably the area that many of us fall short in (Romans 12:12). It is something that I am constantly pulling myself up on. People will often ask me to remember them in prayer, and I glibly say 'Of course I will,' then I forget until the next time I see the person. I am sure that most of us have done this at some time. This is not faithfulness. A part of faithfulness is keeping to the things we say. Keeping our promises.

This was brought home very early in my marriage with Don. I am Don's second wife; because of what he went through in his first marriage he made rather a rash statement one day. He said 'I'll never trust another woman!' I heard it and you can imagine what could have happened in our marriage if I had allowed the words to linger. I determined that I was going to be a woman that he could trust. I did this by ensuring that whenever I said I would do something, I would go out of my way to do it before I next saw him. For instance, if he went off to the office in the morning and he had asked for something to be done before he got home, I would make sure I did it. It took a while for us to work through the problems, but now it is a joy every time I hear Don say that he can trust me. I would never have that joy if I had not been faithful in the little things. This is said very positively in 1 Corinthians 4:2:

> *'Now it is required that those who have been given a trust must prove faithful.'*

Chapter 29

Gentleness

Under this heading I want to deal with four qualities that I feel are very closely linked with each other. They are **gentleness**, **meekness**, **humility** and **submission**. All very different, yet very much entwined with each other.

I have already said a little about the meek and quiet spirit that Timothy exhorts us as women to have. Very much involved with a meek and quiet spirit, is one of the fruits of the Holy Spirit – gentleness (Galatians 5:21–22).

There are many other scriptures which give us more instruction on the subject. Philippians 4:5 tells us that our gentleness must be something that is evident to all. Colossians 3:12 teaches us that as God's chosen people, we are holy and dearly loved, therefore we must clothe ourselves with compassion, kindness, humility, gentleness and patience. Yet another list of qualities for us to build into our lives.

One verse that never ceases to amaze me is the one in 1 Peter 3:15 that tells us that our witnessing must be done with gentleness and respect. Often when we think about witnessing we think about the 'old fashioned' way of street preachers, sandwich-boards and the like; someone pushing the gospel very aggressively. However, I believe that while there is a place for boldness in witnessing, I also believe there is a time when we need to be very wise and our witnessing must be done with gentleness and respect for those we are talking to. I believe there are many more people who are in the Kingdom of God today because of the gentle witness, than because of the aggressive type of witnessing.

One definition of gentleness is to be sensitive. In other words not brash, hard or unfeeling. We are considerate of others. Not aggressive.

This then brings us to the virtues of meekness and humility.

Let us take just a glimpse at the subject of humility. Because we think too highly of ourselves, when we make a mistake and fail, it devastates us and we become knocked out by it. The Bible tells us in Romans 12:3 not think of ourselves more highly than we ought. Because we expect too much of ourselves we often fail.

Developing a humble heart is an on-going process and is an outgrowth of a spirit-filled life. If we seek to fulfil our natural desires, pride will reign in our life. If we stay close to Christ and His purposes, humility will emanate from our hearts and bring glory to our King. Humility is an attitude of the heart.

In Colossians 3:12 and 1 Peter 5:5 we are told that we are to clothe ourselves with humility. It is something that we have to do, no one else will do it for us. God will not do it. God has provided, and all we have to do is to pick up this garment of humility and clothe ourselves with it.

Another verse, James 4:10 tells us that we have to humble ourselves before the Lord. Again we have the thought here that there is something **we** have to do. **We** have to humble ourselves. I am very concerned for people who ask God to humble them. In my reading of the Bible and understanding of God, when He has told us to do something, He expects us to do it.

There is an idea around that in order to be humble, we have to be broken by God. I have never in my reading of the Word of God, come across any verse that gives us any indication that God is in the breaking business. All I read is that God is in the business of creating and making.

There have been many hymns, choruses and songs written about the Potter and the clay, but I will not sing most of them as I do not agree with the sentiments written. Most of the idea is taken from the picture of the Potter and clay in Jeremiah. But to get a full picture we need to read more than just the verses in Jeremiah 18:4 which tells us that because the pot the potter was shaping became marred he formed it into another pot, *'shaping it as seemed best to him.'* The idea here is that as long as the clay is kept soft the potter can make whatever he wishes with the clay. We then turn to Jeremiah 19:11 where God tells Jeremiah to say that He, *'will smash this nation and this city just as this potter's jar is smashed and cannot be repaired.'* Note it says that when the potter's jar is smashed it cannot be repaired. When the clay had dried and set, that is the vessel it will be. There is nothing else that can happen to it, it cannot be remoulded into another vessel. God is in the remoulding business not in the breaking business. As long as we keep ourselves soft and pliable in God's hands then He can make of us whatever He wills. I have met many people who have not wanted God to break them. They have been afraid to surrender themselves totally to God because they have heard others talk about God breaking them. No one in their right mind wants to be broken. I feel that many Christians wish to surrender to the Lord so that they can become whatever He desires, but because of the idea of breaking, they have been unwilling to surrender. When we keep ourselves soft in God's hands, then humility will be something that we can clothe ourselves with willingly, because we know that God will make us a vessel of honour.

The area in which we will see God breaking things, is in the bondages that have come into our lives. Isaiah 10:27 tells us that the yoke will be broken because of the anointing (KJV). The yoke referred to here is in the realm of bondage. God does not break people but He does break bondages in our lives that hold us enslaved. We need to have a broken and contrite heart towards God (Psalm

51:17). Broken because we realise just how much we have hurt God. We must humble ourselves but God will not break us.

Colossians 2:18 talks about false humility. What is false humility? I believe false humility is being humble for the wrong reasons. The thought here in this verse is that false humility is unspiritual, it comes from a mind that wants to think of itself more highly than it ought to think. False humility has wrong ideas of its own importance.

It has been said humility is not in degrading yourself, but in forgetting yourself. Humility is not trying to get the better deal but being content with what God has given us.

In Philippians 2:2–11 Paul makes this stunning statement that our attitude should be the same as Jesus' attitude. I wonder if we have a full understanding of what that attitude was. Jesus humbled Himself we are told, which resulted in His death upon the cross. His humility meant that He left the glory of heaven and came to earth in the form of a man even though He was God himself. In His humility Jesus submitted Himself to God's will. He chose to be humble.

Humility is a choice, it is something we have to do, we make ourselves humble, no one else can do it for us.

Jesus did not belittle Himself, He knew He was the Son of God and yet He still became a servant. Not just a servant to the whole of mankind but more practically to His own disciples. In John 13:1–15 we have the story of Jesus washing His disciple's feet. Then He tells us that He did this to set us an example that we should do likewise, and follow the example of servanthood. Jesus said to Peter that if he did not let Him wash his feet and become his servant, then Peter would have no relationship with Him.

Jesus' disciples asked Him who was the greatest in the Kingdom of God, and His reply was those who were willing to become as humble as a little child (Matthew 18:4). Humility will mean that we are willing to follow Jesus and become a servant. When we are willing to follow that example then we will also see what it cost Jesus to redeem us. That should then give us a better image of ourselves.

We need to put failure behind us, yet at the same time be aware that we are human and that there is still the possibility of failure. Knowing that God loves us we can humbly accept ourselves, follow the example of Jesus and become a real servant. This will result in the freedom to admit our failures. We must have the freedom to fail without becoming a failure.

Humility will involve an accurate assessment of our abilities. This means that we do not over-estimate nor under-estimate ourselves, but we bring ourselves under the control of the Holy Spirit so that the grace of God can operate in our lives.

Involved with humility is meekness, and all that it means.

Matthew 5:5 and Psalm 37:11 tell us that the meek will inherit the earth. What does it mean – the meek will inherit the earth? And what does it mean to be meek?

Many times we have been told that meekness is not weakness. Meekness does not mean that we are trampled on, like a doormat. To be meek only means that we are submissive to whoever is in the place of authority. So to be meek in order to inherit the earth is just another way of saying that we are making God the Lord of our life. We are then living under the rule and reign of Jesus Christ which means we are living in the kingdom of God. Why do we so often think that we need a degree in theology to understand scripture? God wrote the Bible for ordinary people, and once we have accepted Him then He gives us the understanding of His word. We have had many messages that have tried to give us a understanding of meekness. I am convinced that it is more to do with gentleness and humility than anything else. The dictionary definition of meek is 'piously humble and submissive; tamely submissive'. This leads us nicely into the last virtue for this section; that of submission.

I can hear many women expressing surprise that I have

got this far in a book for women and not yet mentioned that dreaded word. The word which we have all cowed under – 'submission'. Well here it is! I do not say I could not write a book for women without mentioning it, but I would say I cannot write a book about the character of a Christian woman without mentioning it because it is a subject which we read about in the Word of God. James 4:7; Hebrews 12:9; Romans 8:7; Job 22:21 all tell us that we need to be submissive to God. One way that we can resist Satan is to first submit to God. I told you at the beginning of the book that when God called me there were a number of scriptures that He gave me. One of these is found in Proverbs 3:5–6:

> *'Trust in the LORD with all your heart and lean not on your own understanding; in all your ways acknowledge Him, and He will make your paths straight.'*

One aspect of submission to God is to acknowledge Him in all that we do. This means that we admit and recognise the Lordship of Christ in our lives. Whatever we are doing we need to have the attitude that Jesus Christ is Lord of our life and it is Him that we are serving and not man. In submitting to God we are saying that we desire God to rule in our life. We are submitting to His will for us.

The next step in submission comes from Ephesians 5:21 and 24 which says we submit to one another out of reverence for Christ just as the church submits to Christ. Hebrews 13:17 instructs us to obey our leaders and submit to their authority because they keep watch over you as men who must give an account. Obey them so that their work will be a joy, not a burden. Of course we can all think of churches around the world that are not in true submission to Christ as Head of the church. If they were, they would not be doing some of the things they are doing. We have to leave that to God to sort out. We must simply obey what God says and be in submission to God and then to one another.

Submission is an attitude of the heart, it is not a gritting of the teeth to see how much of the grace of God we have in our lives. This is an attitude that all of God's children should have. It is **not** just something for a wife or a daughter. It is a requirement for all God's children.

When we truly submit we will also see the virtues of humility, gentleness and meekness demonstrated. Submission is not something that has suddenly occurred in the last decade. It has been in the Word of God from the very beginning. I don't understand why people have to make such a big issue out of it. All of God's children are required by Him to be submissive to Him, to His Son, to the Holy Spirit, to those in authority over them, and to each other. God is not a bad architect and He has built into each one of us the ability to be submissive. Some of us may find it hard because of erroneous teaching, bad example, and worldly ideas that are contrary to the Word of God but that does not annul God's Word. It is clear to me that to be submissive is a characteristic that we must build into our lives if we are truly going to be seen to be children of God.

Chapter 30

Fruits of the Holy Spirit

I want us to look at a few practical points regarding the fruit of the Holy Spirit which should be a part of our character.

Firstly let us look at the fact that fruit usually grows on a tree or bush. Let me put it to you this way. One day you see the fruit tree in your garden writhing around, struggling, and striving with itself. You approach it rather gingerly and the following conversation occurs between you and the tree:

Yourself – 'What are you doing struggling like that?'

Fruit tree – 'Why, don't you know, I am a fruit tree and I am trying hard to bear fruit.'

Yourself – 'But you don't have to struggle to bear fruit. You will bear fruit naturally because you are a fruit tree. There is nothing you have to do. I will do all that is necessary for you to bear fruit. I will water you well. God will give the sunshine to ripen the fruit. All you have to do is stand still and **be**.'

There are many Christians who are struggling to bear fruit, when the reality is that all we have to do is to stand still and see all the provision of God. He has provided us with everything we will need to bear fruit. It will be the natural growth of our life. When the Holy Spirit abides in us then we will bear fruit naturally because it is a part of the life of the Holy Spirit. All that is left for us to do is to yield to the Holy Spirit.

Secondly – a good gardener will always prune his fruit trees. Pruning is done for a number of reasons. To encourage the tree to produce big, good fruit. To stop the growth of wood that will bear no fruit and to help the tree to bear more fruit. Lopping off branches is not very easy. It can be painful especially when we consider that the fruit we have just produced was good fruit. Then the Lord comes along and does some pruning, and we don't understand because all we can see is that the fruit we produced was good.

Thirdly – fruit usually comes in seasons, although today with hypermarkets and supermarkets we can buy almost any kind of fruit at any time. I can remember in my childhood when transportation was not so good and in Cornwall, where we live, we could only get strawberries in June and July. Today we can buy strawberries nearly all the year round. Obviously many of them are imported but nevertheless we can still obtain them whenever we wish. This is not so in real life, the fruit season is according to the fruit. What does this mean for us seeking to produce the fruit of the Holy Spirit? I believe it means that we will bear fruit in the season in which it was meant to be borne. That means that when we need to have the fruit of patience we will be able to produce it. It is no good having joy when we really need patience.

Fourthly – a fruit tree does not devour its own fruit! Fruit is picked and enjoyed by someone other than the tree that produced it. In the same way the fruits of the Holy Spirit in our lives are there not for us to boast about how much fruit we have, but so that others can enjoy our fruit and benefit from it. Therefore each time someone comes and picks a fruit from our tree we will of necessity need to grow another. Because we have been able to produce love for one person it does not mean that love will be automatically there the next time it is needed. We must be careful to produce another crop for the next season. We need to be constantly drawing upon the Holy Spirit in order to have fruit in its season in our lives.

The last few words of Galatians 5:22–23 have dynamic relevance – *'Against such there is no law.'* In other words there are no rules and regulations concerning these fruits. There is complete freedom in producing them and using them.

We cannot produce the fruit of the Spirit by our own effort. There are certain elements we will need in order for us to be able to produce fruit. Good soil, good fertilizer, good sun, a good sap flowing, good watering and good pruning. The words which Jesus spoke in John 15:1–8 need no explanation or expansion. Read them and let the truth of them influence your life.

Chapter 31

Fear

I am positive that most of us have read Proverbs chapter 31. In this chapter we have the description of a woman. If you are like me, after reading it you will feel totally inadequate to emulate this ideal of a perfect woman. Verse 30 I believe gives us hope:

> 'Charm is deceptive, and beauty is fleeting; but a woman who fears the LORD is to be praised.'

One of the main characteristics that I believe we must possess is a fear of the Lord. Verse 29 tells us that many women have done noble things but she surpasses them all. Why does she surpass all the others? I believe it is because she fears God. It is no good us working ourselves to death to build all the characteristics we have looked at into our lives, if we miss this one point. It is better to fear God than to be the most efficient woman in this whole wide world.

Here are some of the women who this verse is referring to:

- **Deborah**: a Judge in Israel (Judges chapter 4). She was a military adviser, a very patriotic woman, one who encouraged Barak in his battles for Israel.
- **Miriam**: the woman who led a nation in praise to God (Exodus 15:20).

141

- **Huldah**: a woman who revealed God's plan to a nation (2 Kings 22).
- **Ruth**: an example of covenant relationship (Ruth).
- **Hannah**: held to be the ideal mother, who gave her child to God (1 Samuel 1).
- **The Shunammite Woman**: we are not even given her name, but she epitomised hospitality (2 Kings 4).
- **Esther**: the woman who risked her life to save God's people (Esther).
- **Sarah** and **Rahab**: both reported to be women of faith (Hebrews 11).
- **Sarah**: the example taken for a submissive wife (1 Peter 3:6).
- **Abigail**: the woman said to be intelligent and beautiful (1 Samuel 25).

Yet when we fear the Lord we will surpass all these notable women who were used by God.

One of the very first things that God told the children of Israel was that they should fear Him (Deuteronomy 10:12). From this verse we see that a right fear of God is closely teamed with our walk with Him. Our personal relationship with God will govern our fear of God. Mention having a personal relationship with God and many women say – 'I can relate to Jesus Christ but I find it difficult to relate to God.' The reason that we may feel like this is because we call God 'Father', and because of our picture of a father we have great difficulty in relating to Him. There are those of us whose father on this earth abused us in some way or other. I believe abuse can be far more than sexual or physical. There is mental abuse, which is a very subtle form of abuse. There are many ministries today who specialize in helping those who have been abused sexually or physically, or both, but there are few who acknowledge even the possibility of mental abuse. Mental abuse can be far more devastating than any other form of abuse because it is so subtle we do not recognise it.

I see mental abuse as an abuse of who we are, our

personality, our ideas, our thoughts, our gifts and talents. To have a child who is gifted in a certain area and not develop that gift is a form of abuse. Another way that we see abuse is when a child is forced to conform to a parent's personal desire for them without any consideration of the child's own desires. I feel that there are more of us who have been subjected to this type of abuse than to the physical or sexual abuse. It may be that one of our parents wanted, as a child, to be a gifted pianist but never made it, so that when we were born their one ambition was to make us what they could never be. Then when it becomes clear that we have no such gift, we can become rebellious, as a reaction against the dominant father. When we become a Christian and we are told to relate to God as Father, we can only see the domination of our earthly father and so we shy away from a deep relationship with Him.

We can then have the situation where a father is only seen as one who punishes you for wrong-doing. This can happen when the role of a father is only portrayed as the one who corrects and punishes for misbehaviour and there has been no affection or love shown while growing up. When this occurs, all we can see God as, is someone with a big stick waiting for us to do wrong and punish us. We find it very hard to see God as He is portrayed in the Bible; one who desires us to relate to Him in love and to receive all that He has provided for us.

On the opposite side we can have people who only see God as a provider, because while they were in their parent's household, father was the one who provided the money for everything they wanted. Nothing was denied them, and they were never told '**no**'! So when this type of person becomes a Christian, they see God as a provider who gives them everything they want and denies them nothing. They have a hard time then relating to the God of the Bible who is shown as a God of judgement and as a God of love. These people seem to be able to highlight all the scriptures that tell us we can have whatever we ask for in the name of Jesus. They appear to ignore those that contain the aspect of parenthood that denies a child something it wants which is not good for it to have. At that time, perhaps they would not know how to handle it, or maybe it just is not good for them to continually have all they see and want! Good parenting is a balance of love with affection, correction with discipline and punishment with encouragement. Why should God be any different with His children? God is the perfect Father. God is the model Father. When God does not answer our prayer just as we want Him to, we quickly feel that He is rejecting us, denying us something that is good for us, or not loving us. In reality He is just being a good Father in knowing what is right for us at this time.

Then there is the type of mental abuse found in some parts of the world, though not all, which impresses upon us that because we are female we are only good for mundane tasks and giving birth. The reasoning behind this abuse is the idea that women have no capacity for intelligent thought and conversation. Like some Jewish men who thank God every morning that He did not make them a woman! Some have grown up with a shadow over them that they are worthless because they are female. This form of abuse is devastating and it can take a long time to get free from it.

Whatever kind of abuse we feel that we have been put through there is freedom for us when we turn to God. Most types of abuse will result in fear controlling us, and God does not want us to live in that fear.

The longer I am a Christian the more I realise that we are worshipping a God that we truly do not fully understand. This should not stop us from worshipping Him, but should make us more determined to seek to know Him so that we do understand Him more.

When reading the Bible I often try to put myself in the place of the Bible characters, trying to see through their eyes, and I nearly always reach the conclusion that if I were in their shoes I certainly would not have understood what God was trying to do at that point in time. We now have the advantage of the end of the stories and can clearly see what God was doing in the situations concerned. So it is with our lives; we cannot see the future, we do not know the end of our time, all we can do is to submit to what is taking place at this time. We need to trust that God is in control and that He has my best interests at heart. Only He knows the end from the beginning, therefore He knows what is best for me. This trust will bring us security for the future. What it really boils down to is a complete surrender to the will and purpose of God in our life.

Satan said to God about Job *'Does Job fear God for nothing?'* (Job 1:9) Even Satan recognised that when a man has the right fear of God then there are many positive things that happen in his life.

The following scriptures give us some of the things which we can expect from God when we fear Him: Psalm 25:14; Psalm 34:7; Psalm 34:9; Psalm 103:11; Psalm 147:11; Proverbs 10:27. There are many other scriptures that teach us about the fear of the Lord. If you do not have a good or a right fear of the Lord, then I would suggest that you do a Bible study and go through the Word of God looking up every scripture that talks about the fear of God. Many scriptures tell us that the fear of the Lord is the very beginning of our relationship with Him. If it has not been a part of our relationship with God, then I cannot urge you enough to start from now on and begin to teach yourselves the fear of the Lord, for no one else can do it for us. This is yet another of those things we have to teach ourselves (Psalm 111:10; Proverbs 1:7).

There is another attribute to the fear of the Lord that I consider important to us. It is that we should hate anything that is evil or anything to do with evil (Proverbs 8:13). A right fear of the Lord will keep us from the snares of sin that lead to death. When we have a fear of the Lord, then anything that has even the sniff of being wrong, sinful and evil will be something that we will abhor (Proverbs

14:27; Proverbs 16:6). Fear of the Lord will give us a strength with which to resist evil, for we will know that it displeases our Lord (Job 28:28).

This then brings us to the end of the matter – for we are told in Ecclesiates 12:13:

> '... *here is the conclusion of the matter: Fear God and keep His commandments, for this is the whole duty of man.*'

If we truly mean business with God then I know He will help us, and the Prayer of David in Psalm 86:11 is a good place to start:

> '*Teach me your way, O LORD, and I will walk in your truth; give me an undivided heart, that I may fear your name.*'

Chapter 32

Wisdom

The Bible has quite a lot to teach us about wisdom, some in conjunction with fear. Psalm 111:10 tells us that:

'The fear of the LORD is the beginning of wisdom.'

If we wish to have wisdom then it will begin with a right fear of God. What does it mean to be wise, or to have wisdom? Wisdom means – discernment, insight, judgment, sense, discretion. All of these characteristics I am sure we would love to possess.

When we begin to think about wisdom, it is most likely that all of us will think of one man from the Bible – Solomon. A man who has the reputation of being the wisest man who ever lived! I am not sure he deserved that reputation at the end of his days, for he was disobedient to God and married many foreign wives who turned his heart away from God. I am sure that there is no wisdom in being disobedient to what God says to us. Solomon, the King of Israel asked God for wisdom to rule God's people. God gave him wisdom, and we can read much of his wise counsel and decisions in the Word of God (2 Chronicles 1:10–12; 1 Kings 4:29; 1 Kings 5:12; 1 Kings 10:24). Our wisdom will begin with being obedient to what we hear God say to us.

In order to live a life that will please God we need to carefully watch what we are doing with our time and our days (Psalm 90:12). The prayer of the Psalmist asks God to teach him how to take account of his time so that he could gain wisdom. Many of us wish we had far more time, but each one of us has the same amount of time given to us. We all have twenty-four hours in every day, seven days in every week and fifty-two weeks in every year in which to live our lives. Each one of us will choose what we do with that time and how we fill it.

One of my hobbies is needlecraft. Give me a needle, thread and some cloth and I will be happy for hours. It is something that I enjoy and any spare moment you can find me with some kind of needle in my hand. Many people, when they discover the things I do, say they do not know where I get the time. My usual reply is that you always make time for the things you want to do. Ephesians 5:16 tells us to make the most of every opportunity. Our time is our own and how we use that time will determine what we accomplish in this life. Wisdom from God will not just come as we make careful use of our time, but will also give us more wisdom on how to use our time.

God has told us that if we lack wisdom then we should ask Him and He will give it to us (James 1:5). James also gives us some insight into how we can discern what wisdom is. In James 3:17 we have some good guidelines to help us to discern if we ourselves are wise, but also if the counsel we are getting from others is God's wisdom or worldly wisdom. The questions to ask are these:

- Is this advice pure?
- Is it holy, godly, unselfish, free from wrong motives?
- Is it going to make peace or will it stir up contention?.
- Is it considerate of everyone involved?
- Does it point me towards submission to God's will, or will it be just pleasing man?
- Will it bear good fruit?
- Is it full of mercy?
- Is it impartial, or will it be pandering to someone else's desires?
- Is it sincere?

Wisdom probably is not what most of us thought it to be. We must not shy away from it thinking that we will be 'bothered' by others if we become wise. We must seek to develop wisdom in our character so that we become wise.

Another aspect from scripture I want us to look at that applies especially to us as women, is found in Proverbs 14:1:

> *'The wise woman builds her house, but with her own hands the foolish one tears hers down.'*

What does this mean for us today?

When we think about a house, we usually think about a place in which we live. It can be a shelter, or it may be a palace, a mud hut, a bamboo shack, a flat, tenement building, a detached house, or a bungalow. It is a place of security. A place where you live, where you have possessions, however much or little. The aspect I want us to look at, is that it is a place of security. A place where we can be ourselves, where we are at home.

No matter what our culture, every human being needs to know that they have a place where they belong. According to our verse if we are wise we will build that place, but if we are foolish we will tear it down.

When we are wise, we will be able to build this place where we can be known for who we are. A place where we can be ourselves, and live in security knowing that we are accepted. One of the major aspects of this security will be in our relationship with God. If we truly know that God accepts us and loves us then we will be secure no matter where we are.

Every human being needs to know this place of security. It will not come suddenly, but it will be developed as we grow in our relationship with God. This will also mean that we will grow in our security as people. No one likes uncertainty. No one likes to be in the place where they are unsure of what is happening. We all like to be sure of what is going on around us. The one place that we can find this place of certainty is in God.

The only thing at this point in time I can be certain of, is that God is in complete control and He knows what is happening to me and what will happen in my life. I can therefore rest secure because of what I know of God. There have been quite a few changes in the circumstances of my life in the past few years and it would appear that there are more to come, but I feel I can face them positively because I know an assurance and security in my relationship with God that tells me no matter what happens, I am secure in Him and He will help me face every situation.

As I told you, I felt God called me to the ministry of 'helps' and because of this, I have developed an attitude that whatever I felt God asking me to do He would give me all that I needed to fulfil it. I believe that whoever God calls He will also equip. God will not call you to something that He will not give you the ability to fulfil. So every situation I find myself in I look to God for His strengthening to do it. This has meant that over the years I have been called to do almost every job you can think of! There was a time in our team ministry when I was the soloist, another time I was the organist. At one time I was the secretary! I have prepared and edited numerous editions of our publications. I have also been and still am the person responsible for the accounts of Good News Crusade (this is the official body that carries our ministry). I have put up tents. I have been the chief cook and bottle washer! I have run the children's work. I will not list any more, but this is just to let you know that where my faith has reached out to God He has also met me. This does not mean that at times when I face a situation I do not feel inadequate. I do, quite often, but then I look to God and I soon discover that He is with me. There are times because I talk positively this way, that people say to me:

'It seems as though you have lived a charmed life.'

'Does nothing ever go wrong for you?'

'Don't you ever find that life is dealing you a bad deal?'

To answer truthfully I can say that there are times when I become frustrated and wish that things were different. Times when I would rather not face what I am having to face. But I can also truthfully say when I look back on those times, all I can see is how God brought me and Don through together. I can only see the victories.

In the early days of our ministry there were times when we did not have enough to eat. On occasions we were down to our last penny. Other times we did not know where the money was going to come from to clothe the children. I can even remember a time when I pawned a silver bracelet in order to buy petrol to get us to our next crusade! All I can see looking back is the way in which God undertook for us. We are not special people. You have the same supply available to you. All of God's children are give the same inheritance in Christ, the only difference is that some of us have claimed that inheritance and others are still grovelling around in the dust unaware of what is theirs.

This reminds me of a story I heard many many years ago about a lady who lived in Africa. Her son had gone overseas to work and every month he sent her a gift from his wage packet. This lady living in the African bush had never seen paper money, and did not know what it was that her son was sending her. All she thought of was the nice picture of the people on the pieces of pretty coloured paper that her son kept sending her! This continued for some years. One day a European missionary visited her mud hut and was surprised to see her walls covered with all this paper money. There were five pound notes, ten pound notes, and old ten shilling notes. The missionary through an interpreter, explained what these 'nice pictures' were, took the money to a local town and had it changed into the local currency. The lady then became the richest lady in the whole area! She was rich before she knew she was rich. She lived in poverty not knowing what her son had provided for her. What an excellent illustration for so many in God's kingdom. We are the richest people around, yet so many of us are living in spiritual poverty because we do not claim what God has given us. We live with nice 'pictures' in our Bible and in our thoughts, but we do not make them reality.

From very early in my walk with God I have been taught that God is sovereign, that He is a covenant-keeping God. What God has said He will do, He will do, there is no doubt about it. God made promises to men, to nations, or groups of people, and they were fulfilled. That is what I have discovered as I have read my Bible. Many of these promises were made by covenant. Covenant today in our western society is something we don't fully appreciate or understand. If we are going to fully understand the Bible we need to have a good understanding of covenant, for we will never fully be able to appreciate God and His promises until we have a full grasp of what covenant is. Covenant has been said to be a final, irrevocable commitment. God dealt with His people by covenant. He made covenant with Abraham, Noah, the children of Israel, David and us through the New Covenant.

God does not change His mind (Malachi 3:6; Hebrews 7:21; James 1:17). God keeps His promises (2 Corinthians 1:20). God does not say one thing and mean another. We still have the evidence today of the very first covenant which God made with the whole of creation in Genesis 9. In verse 13 God said:

'I have set my rainbow in the clouds, and it will be the sign of the covenant between me and the earth.'

Every time I see a rainbow I declare that my God is a God who keeps His promises. Because of this fact I can rest secure knowing that the God who I have come to know over the past years is a God who keeps His promises. I have an assurance that He knows what is best for me therefore I am secure. In other words I have built my house, I have a secure place from which I can work from. That security comes from my relationship with God and no matter where I am in the world, I am secure. My house is not where I live in St. Austell, Cornwall, in the kingdom of Great Britain. My house in the Kingdom of God. That is where I live. Since I have been born again into a new kingdom this is where I draw my security from.

When we have found and built this place in our relationship with God then out from that place we will be able to build friendships with others. We will be able to give to others out of the security of a firm foundation.

How do we become foolish and tear this place down? The number one way is by negatives, by listening to the 'wisdom' of the world that constantly bombards women with thoughts of equal rights or degrades the position of women to second-class citizenship. We no longer live in this world. We who are born again live in the Kingdom of God and that means we are in Christ, which means that there is no male or female (Galatians 3:28). It would appear that most Christian people believe that the down-grading of women came from the Hebrew culture of the Bible. (During our many visits to Israel I discovered that the Hebrew view of women is far from what we have been led to believe. Before the time of the early New Testament Church there was no segregation in the synagogues of women and men. This segregation only came about during the New Testament Church era. Hebrew women were well looked after, highly thought of and respected. After all, it was only through them that the nation would continue! Still today the Jewish line is continued through the mothers' lineage.)

When we start listening to negative thinking it down-grades us as women and soon these seeds that are planted into our lives will grow and mature, until before long we believe them and we ourselves become negative. What greater position is there in this life than to be called a child of God? I feel down-graded when I hear the world talking about equal rights for women, etc. The only right

I want is to be called a child of God. Jesus tells us in John 1:12 that to all who received Him, to those who believed in His name, He gave the right to become children of God. Because I am the child of the King I can hold my head high, for I am a citizen of a Kingdom that is going to last for ever. The whole definition of 'kingdom' means the rule and reign of the life of the 'king', and my King will never die. So let us build that place of security and no longer listen to those that would tear down our place and our position in God's Kingdom for that is not wisdom that comes from above.

Chapter 33

Confidence and Boldness

When we hear people say of someone, 'She's very confident,' do we ask ourselves, 'I wonder what makes her so confident?'

Confidence should be a characteristic that is found in every Christian. It is important that our confidence is based on the right foundation. Our confidence should not be in ourselves but our confidence should come out of our relationship with God.

Many people put their confidence in how they appear to others, depending upon what they wear and how they look, instead of depending upon the inner purity of spirit. Confidence goes far deeper than the outward show. True confidence begins in our heart. Knowing with assurance that we are born again and a child of God, we then have the power and the right to live in confidence (John 1:12–13).

If we are going to be truly confident then I believe we need to start at the beginning and that is by being honest about ourselves. In 2 Corinthians 13:5 Paul tells us that we should examine ourselves to see whether or not we are in the faith. We have to test ourselves. We can start by:

(a) being honest with ourselves,
(b) beginning to understand ourselves, and
(c) acknowledging what we are.

It takes courage to look into ourselves in this way, discovering why we do the things we do, or react in the way we do.

Consider your family, your upbringing, your schooling, your environment, your culture, your friends, all have contributed to who you are as a person. Some of you may feel that there are a 'whole bunch' of negatives in your background, and that you live under the circumstances instead of on top of them. You feel a victim of all of these things therefore you lack confidence because you feel you have nothing to be confident in. There are probably things you do not like about your past, family, school, or friends. Things you would very much like to change, things you wish had not been part of your life.

Confidence will only truly come when you accept who and what you are. Perhaps there are many negatives in your past and in your life today, but acknowledging them and accepting them as part of you will help you to change yourself. Maybe, because of your past, you feel unable to really like yourself. The Bible tells us that we should not only like ourselves but in fact we must love ourselves. This means an acceptance of who we are and who God has made us. It implies that if we cannot love ourselves we won't ever be able to love our neighbours (Mark 12:28–31). Most of us have difficulty loving some of our neighbours and it may be because we have not yet begun to love and accept ourselves. Please note it is love your neighbour **as** yourself, not as you love God. You will never be able to really love your neighbours, and that includes your brothers and sisters in the church of God, until you start to love yourself. Accept who you are with confidence.

It was Martin Luther who said that God does not love that which is worthy of love, but God's love creates that which is worthy of being loved.

God lives within you. God has created within you something worthy of being loved and that is the life of Jesus. Therefore do not insult God by not loving what He has created to be loved. God loved you enough to send Jesus to die for you, so you can begin loving yourself on that basis alone. This is not a selfish love (which we have already considered).

Begin by building confidence in who God has made you. As I said, confidence comes from your heart and your heart attitudes. Confidence will come out of your relationship with God.

There are people in our world today who gain confidence from what they have made of themselves. They put their confidence in their career, the position they have reached in their firm, business, or job; in the money they earn or have inherited. It could even be in who their parents are. This type of person does not really have true confidence. Many of them end up disillusioned with life, divorce their partner, or even commit suicide, because they feel fed up with their life. This is not true confidence; that comes from knowing who we are. Who are we? A son of God! So that is where we draw our confidence from (Ephesians 3:12; 1 Corinthians 3:4). Confidence comes through the work of Christ. Our confidence is in Him in us. Once we truly know that we are 'in Christ' then we can have confidence to come before God. To come into His presence with boldness because we know that He will accept us because of His Son.

We read in Hebrews 10:35 that confidence is something we can discard. By an act of our will we can determine to be confident or not. We will have that choice to make in every situation we find ourselves in. That choice will then determine if we face the situation in confidence or in fear. When you know in your heart that you are in Christ, and that Christ is in you, you can face whatever approaches you with confidence.

It is like the illustration often told of the little girl who was asked to give her testimony. She very timidly told how she had heard Jesus knocking on the door of her heart and she had asked Him to come into her life. She was then asked the question, 'Did Jesus come?' She replied very confidently that He had. The next question came, 'What

157

happened next?' She said that the next day there was another knock on the door. 'Who was it this time?' she was asked. 'Well,' she said, 'when I looked I saw that it was Satan.' 'Oh, and what did you do then?' 'I asked Jesus to answer the door!' She knew with a certainty that Jesus had come into her life and that He was living within her. This is the confidence that we need. An assurance that Christ lives in us. So then with confidence we can not only ask Him to answer the door when Satan calls but also know that we can face every situation knowing that He is in us.

We can gain confidence by positive confession (2 Chronicles 32:8). That confession must be based upon what God has said. God has told us that He is not only with us but that His Spirit dwells in us. A positive confession of who lives within us will boost our confidence.

Our confidence can become secure and unwavering when it is based upon God, and when it is in the right place (Proverbs 3:26). When our confidence is in the right place then we will not fall nor fail. Confidence is a direct result of knowing our position in Christ.

Ninety times in his epistles Paul gave reference to our being 'in Christ' (Romans 6:11; 1 Corinthians 1:2; 1 Corinthians 1:4; 2 Corinthians 1:21; Ephesians 2:6).

We are told that once we become a child of God His righteousness will produce confidence (Isaiah 32:17). Confidence will be evidence that we have received the righteousness of God. But how do we become righteous?

Righteousness comes by faith. That faith is in Christ. It is also a gift from God; we can do nothing to earn it (Romans 3:22; Romans 5:17). It is not a reward for doing good. It is not a prize for attaining some special goal. It is not a presentation gift for long service. It is a gift given to us by God when we accept the life offered to us by Jesus Christ. Knowing our position in Christ – which is complete and perfect – will produce that righteousness which in turn will also give us confidence.

When our confidence is truly in the Lord then we will be

blessed (Jeremiah 17:7). What is this word 'blessed'? As Christians we use it often. What do we mean by it and what does the word of God mean by it? Blessed is the word Jesus used in His famous Sermon on the Mount. The Sermon on the Mount is a series of statements which are known today as the Beatitudes. Each one starts with the word 'blessed'. According to the dictionary it means to be blissful, joyous, holy, happy. So this is what we can be when we gain our confidence.

Paul says very clearly that we must put no confidence in the flesh (Philippians 3:3-4). Even if we do have some natural reason to be confident we can really put no confidence in it. Paul had every reason to have confidence in his natural standing before man, but he is teaching us that we should only allow our confidence to come from God.

As we see in Hebrews 4:14-16, we have a High Priest who has gone before us, who had been through all that we have, yet He did not sin; so because of this we can come before God with confidence. The reason we can do this is because of the blood of Jesus Christ (Hebrews 10:19). Another reason for our confidence is when we have a clear conscience before God (1 John 3:21), and we know of nothing in our life God has spoken to us about that is unfulfilled. When there is nothing that we have knowingly been disobedient about, and we are walking in the light, and we can be confident. All these point us in one direction – our relationship to God. What we know of God in our lives will give us confidence. What we know of God through His Word will give us confidence. An aspect of confidence can be boldness. When the disciples and those in the upper room were filled with the Holy Spirit, we are told that they received boldness. They had been hiding away out of fear but now they came into the open with a confidence and boldness that they did not have before. One of the prayers of the early church was that they would have boldness to speak God's Word (Acts 4:29). Boldness means to be brave and intrepid. One person from the Bible who would fit this description is Peter.

Peter was so bold that sometimes he was taken wrongly. Jesus had to rebuke Peter for his boldness in speaking out (Matthew 16:23). It was Peter who took Jesus at his word and walked on water (Matthew 14:29). Yet it was also Peter who was the first one on his feet after the day of Pentecost to bear witness and testify about the Holy Spirit and the tongues of fire! (Acts 1:15). So we see in Peter the boldness that can either be human impetuousness or a Spirit-filled bravery, which came out of confidence because of what the Holy Spirit had done in his life.

Confidence and boldness are characteristics that we will need in our lives to stand up for God in our communities. Confidence will not always be manifested by boldness. On occasions our confidence could mean that we keep quiet and do not openly speak out. Sometimes to keep quiet is better than being so bold that it comes out aggressively.

In no way do I want you to think that I have covered every virtue and character of a Christian. I have only taken those that I felt the Lord direct me to. In closing this section I wish to end with one characteristic that I feel covers all others. I say this because without this characteristic in our lives, we will quickly become ship-wrecked.

Chapter 34

Discernment

We read in 1 Corinthians 2:14–15 that,

> *'The man without the Spirit does not accept the things
> that come from the Spirit of God, for they are foolish-
> ness to him, and he cannot understand them, because
> they are spiritually discerned. The spiritual man makes
> judgments about all things, but he himself is not subject
> to any man's judgment.'*

It is of vital importance that we know how to discern the
things that come from the Spirit of God and those that do
not. I never cease to be amazed at the statement that Jesus
made in Matthew 24:24:

> *'For false Christs and false prophets will appear and
> perform great signs and miracles to deceive even the
> elect – if that were possible.'*

I am so glad that He ended with those words, *'If that were
possible.'* I often comfort myself with that thought. Once
we have been born-again by the Spirit of God and have
been filled with His Holy Spirit we are a 'spiritual man'.
So long as we keep our relationship with God alive, and
are sensitive to His Spirit we will be able to discern. Do

not be deceived by the devil or anyone else, allow the Spirit of God to give you discernment, and use it.

The mature – those who have grown in their Christian life – are those who can take solid food, and have trained themselves to discern good and evil (Philippians 1:9–10; Hebrews 5:14). The question we need to ask ourselves then is: have we trained ourselves? Are we mature? Can we take solid food?

Some of the wisdom from Proverbs 3:21 is very relevant to this point, when the preacher advises his son to preserve sound judgment and discernment, and not let them out of his sight. Discernment will be vital to each one of us. Some Christians call it 'the witness of the Spirit'. Whatever it is called, it is there for each one of us once we know the Spirit of God, so do not be deceived, but seek God for discernment. In 1 Corinthians 12 we have a list of gifts that the Holy Spirit gives, and among them is the ability to distinguish between spirits. Notice it is a small 's', meaning all spirits other than the Holy Spirit. We should be able to discern between a human spirit, an evil spirit and the Holy Spirit. It is necessary for us to be able to identify all three.

Why do I say that we need to have discernment? Because we have to be able to discern in our own spirit where we ourselves are coming from; our thoughts, our motivations, the words we feel come to us. Are they from our spirit, an evil spirit or the Spirit of God?

We have the instruction in 1 John 4:1 that we should not believe every spirit, but must test the spirits to see whether they are from God, because many false prophets have gone out into the world. If Paul was writing this today he would probably say something like this – 'Stop believing everything you hear, but start to be selective; begin to think about what you are hearing!'

For those of us who believe that we are living in the 'last days', when the second coming of Jesus Christ is near, it is of vital importance that we exercise discernment. The Bible tells us that there will be many false prophets in the 'last days' (Matthew 7:15; Matthew 24:11, 24; Mark 13:22; 1 John 4:1). In order to be able to know if they are false or not we need to have discernment. This again will come out of our relationship with God. When His Spirit is indwelling us we have the potential of true discernment. Sometimes this will mean not listening to all the popular ideas and teachings that are the 'in' thing at the moment, but listening to what we hear God saying to us in our hearts, knowing His voice.

PART THREE

The Victorious Life of a Godly Woman

Chapter 35

Recognising the Enemy

Anyone who has ever tried to live the Christian life will tell you they had not been a Christian very long before they discovered they were in a personal battle. If we believe that we are in a battle then we need to know who our enemy is, what his strength is, what his tactics are, and then how to defeat him. I want to cover all these areas in an attempt to help you walk with God in victory. He has given us all we need to enable us to walk in victory. In Hosea 4:6 we are told that we will be destroyed if we lack knowledge, and part of this knowledge is about our enemy so that we can defeat him. There are many passages in the Bible that teach us that it is God's will for us to live in victory (1 Corinthians 15:57; 1 John 5:4; Psalm 44:7; Proverbs 2:7).

Nowhere in the Bible are we given a clear explanation of who Satan is, or how he got here. It simply assumes his existence. Most Bible scholars and theologians appear to believe that in Ezekiel 28 there is possibly a reference to him. One thing is very clear from scripture; we do have a spiritual enemy.

There are some people who do not believe that the devil is our enemy. Others believe that he is not real. Jesus spoke about him and gave us some insight to help us. We also know that Jesus was tempted by the devil. One of the main tactics of the devil is to tempt us, but scripture clearly tells us that because Jesus was tempted and overcame him, so can we (Matthew 4:1; Hebrews 4:15; Hebrews 2:18).

In Matthew 13:38–39 Jesus is explaining one of His parables to His disciples. He makes it very clear that there are two kinds of seeds that are sown, one is good and the other is bad. He calls the latter weeds. Both are sown together, but one is sown by God and the other is sown by the enemy, who is the devil. So Jesus was under no illusion that we have an enemy who is working against us. He gives us further insight in Luke 10:19. Here He is telling us that we have authority over all the power of the enemy, and that there is nothing which he can bring against us that can harm us. Yet many of us live under the influence of the enemy's power, thinking that there is nothing we can do about it. In 1 Peter 5:8 we are given a picture of the enemy as a lion, walking around looking for people to pounce on and destroy, and who else would he wish to destroy but his enemy's people! The object of a battle is to destroy the opposition.

When the devil tempted Jesus to fall down and worship him in exchange for all the kingdoms of the earth, it would appear that he was acting out his ambition to be God and rule the world. We know that this ambition is one that he will never accomplish. Nevertheless he will do all in his power to try and diminish his enemy's people, to make them weak, and to immobilise them. He also knows that his time is limited. In fact, the Bible calls it 'short' (Revelation 12:12). As long as the devil is around we will be engaged in spiritual warfare. It is a fact of life, for the final victory of the Kingdom of God is in the future. This is when the devil will be destroyed.

Some people ask the question: 'If God is so powerful and the devil so bad why does God allow him still to exist?' God's sovereignty over the world cannot be questioned. God allows Satan to exist and to operate in the world knowing that He has already defeated him.

Paul gives us a little more insight. In 2 Corinthians 2:11 he writes these words:

> '... *in order that Satan might not outwit us. For we are not unaware of his schemes.*'

The biggest problem we have is that a large percentage of God's people are unaware of his schemes and he does outwit them. My goal is to redress this position. The first thing we need to establish is what Satan wishes to accomplish. I believe there are three clear main thrusts of Satan's work:

1. To keep unbelievers in the dark (2 Corinthians 4:4; Matthew 13:19);
2. To make believers spiritually ineffective. As believers we are in the position to bring glory to God and this is something that Satan has committed himself to prevent (Romans 15:6; Mark 7:13);
3. To hinder the work of God in the world. In 1 Thessalonians 2:18 Paul says that many times he wanted to go to them but Satan had hindered him. Again in Romans 15:22 Paul says he was hindered from coming to them. Satan will try and stop the Word of God because he knows the power it holds.

The main passage of scripture to assist us in our spiritual battle is Ephesians 6:10–18 and I am sure that most of us, if not all of us, have heard a message, tape, seminar or read something about it. So it is not my intention to give any explanation of this passage, but to mention that the armour which God has supplied for us is total. I want to look at some of the subtle things which Satan uses as his battle tactics to try and defeat us in our personal life.

Chapter 36

Tactics Satan Uses

Deceit and Lies

Ever since Satan appeared on the scene he has been a liar and deceiver (John 8:44; 2 Corinthians 11:3). Satan's very first appearance was one when he deceived and lied. Jesus is very clear that whenever the devil speaks he does so out of his own nature which is to tell lies.

When we enter a battle, if the enemy openly attacks us then it is easy for us to defend ourselves.

When the enemy comes against us with a temptation we can make a choice to submit to God, or to submit to the temptation (James 4:7). Our first point is to submit to God. We will never be able to resist the devil if we do not first submit to God.

When the enemy comes to us to tell us lies and deceive us we don't even know that anything is wrong. This is the whole nature of deception.

Many people give the devil power that in reality he does not have. Fear of the devil will make him attack us even more. In my own experience and also in listening to people's testimonies it would appear that there are four main times that the devil will attack us,

(a) when we are alone,
(b) when it is dark,
(c) when we are in a weak condition physically,
(d) when we are in a weak condition spiritually.

When we are in these positions we should be extra

vigilant, being aware that it is at these times when we are most vulnerable to the attack of our enemy.

Often Satan deceives by offering power to deal with problems. This he will do by telling us we can do it by ourselves, in our own strength, and acting independently of God; or we can use the occult, mediumistic spirits, witchcraft etc. He promises power but only gives strength to keep his victims coming back. His charges are very high, and usually take the form of bondage in some area of the person's life. Satan will try and deceive us about spiritual truths, by offering us false doctrines (2 Corinthians 11:13).

He will also deceive us about the character of God and about our identity as a child of God (1 Timothy 4:1). Once a person's concept of God has been perverted, the concept of what it means to be a child of God is affected. We can end up blaming God for all the bad things which happen in our lives, and believe that we have to reach a certain level of holiness before God will accept us.

He will also deceive us about spiritual truths. He will try to get us out of balance and tied up with trivia. One of the easiest tactics he uses with many churches and Christians is to keep them focused on the death of Jesus, instead of looking at the resurrection, which gives us life and power, and is the real purpose of His death.

One year while my husband and I were on holiday we visited some underground caves. When we were about half-way through our guide told us that we would soon be coming to a place in the caves that was very dangerous. She explained that we would come to an edge of a cliff, and the drop over the cliff was about twenty kilometres. She warned parents to be sure to keep their children away, and joked that this was the place to push your husband or wife over if you were fed up with them! We rounded a corner, and there in front of us was this large hole. The dimensions seemed to be about twelve feet by eight feet. Our guide asked a man to take a large stone and throw it into the hole so we could hear the echo. The gentleman very obligingly did as he was asked. Can you imagine the reactions when the stone hit water? The lighting in the caves was so placed, that what looked like a large cliff with a very deep fall was in fact only a pool of approximately twenty centimetres! Because there was no wind inside the caves, the pool's surface was totally undisturbed and reflected the lighting perfectly to give the illusion. To me this illustrates very vividly how easily we can be deceived. No matter how perfect the deception is, when we are faced with the truth the deception is seen for what it is. Then when the truth is seen all the fear and apprehension goes.

Let us not be ignorant as to how Satan can outwit and deceive us.

Another subtle form of deception is self-deception. The Bible clearly tells us that it is possible to have self-deception (1 Corinthians 3:18; James 1:22; 1 John 1:8). This can take many different forms. One interesting passage in Titus 3:3 says that our emotions can deceive us. Just when we feel we have gained a victory over other kinds of deception, Satan comes and deceives us with self-deception. This often takes the form of deceiving us about where we are in our relationship with God. Using our own emotions (feelings) Satan will convince us that we are doing alright and that our relationship with God is just fine, when in reality there is much to be desired. This is why we need the helmet of salvation spoken of in Ephesians 6 to protect our minds from deception.

Accusation

Another of the tactics which Satan uses in a Christian's life is that of accusation. Satan will accuse us of various things; that we have not prayed enough, read our Bibles enough, sought God enough, attended church enough. He will accuse us of sin which we have not committed. He will accuse us of anything and everything he can.

In Revelation 12:10 Satan is called the *'accuser of our brothers.'* One positive reaction when Satan accuses us is to say – 'Thank you Satan for just confirming that I am a child of God!' For it says he accuses the brothers!

It is important for us to realise that when God convicts of sin He shows us how to deal with that sin through the cross of Jesus Christ. However when Satan accuses us, he does it to discourage and try to make us give up. Accusation is one of the most subtle tactics Satan will use. Very often an accusation comes close to something that we already have a problem with and are trying to overcome. He accuses us, and tries to make us believe we are condemned by God who will not forgive us. His accusation is usually near the truth, which is why we so easily believe him.

Weaknesses

Satan will always try to capitalise on our weaknesses (Romans 8:26; 2 Corinthians 12:9). Weakness is not sin! Weakness is an area that we can prove God's power in. For we read in the above scripture that His power is made perfect in our weakness. Satan will try and attack us when we are weak, for it is when we are at our weakest point that we are vulnerable. We must be aware that this is the time Satan will try and attack us and when we feel weak we must consciously draw upon God's power and His Spirit to help us.

One thing that we must remember that will help us to draw upon God's help, is found in 1 Corinthians 10:13. It tells us that everything we are tempted with is common to man, and that God is faithful; He will not let you be tempted beyond what you can bear. But when you are tempted, He will also provide a way out so that you can stand up under it. God has given us this promise of an escape route whenever we are tempted.

Division

Another of Satan's ways is to cause division. God always brings union and harmony, but Satan will always bring confusion and division. So wherever you find division you will find Satan at work and wherever you find unity you can be sure God is at work. This is especially true when we come to the church and family. Satan deceived Adam and Eve and brought division between them and he has been attempting to do the same ever since. One of Satan's most successful tactics in our world today is to bring division to the families in God's church. Dividing husband and wife, parents and children.

God says very clearly that husband and wife are one and that no man should try and separate what God has joined (Matthew 19:6). Satan will use anything to divide husband and wife. We must be aware in our marriages that Satan desires to bring division. Also within families and with friends, Satan will always be trying to divide (Matthew 10:21, 36). Many Christians have taken the verses from Matthew 10:21 and 36 to justify a divided family situation, but I do not feel that what these verses are teaching is that the gospel will cause 'Christian' families to be divided. What it is saying is that there will be division within families when a member of the family becomes a Christian and the other members of the family turn their backs on the gospel. When we are Christians the Word of God is constantly urging us to *'keep the unity of the faith'* (Romans 15:5; Ephesians 4:3; Colossians 3:14).

When we read these scriptures we clearly see that the goals for each of us are the unity of the faith, and the unity of the Spirit, not division. We must become wise about Satan's desire to bring division and do all in our power to stop him dividing our families, friendships and church.

Footholds

Ephesians 4:26–31 opens with the statement *'In your anger do not sin'* and do not let the sun go down while you are still angry, then comes this amazing statement in verse

27 which says *'and do not give the devil a foothold.'* Notice that it is us who gives the devil the foothold. It does not say that he will take it by force, but that we yield to him. When our anger allows us to sin then we have given the devil one of those footholds. A foothold is something that anyone climbing a mountain is constantly on the look-out for. Without the right footholds it would be impossible to climb some rock faces. But once you have a foothold it is easy to push yourself up to look for another, then another, until you have climbed to the peak. I believe that this is exactly the thinking behind this scripture. Once we give the devil one such foothold into our life he can quickly and easily find another, and before we know where we are he has an inroad into our life. Do not be deceived. The devil will find the smallest foothold to start with. The passage then goes on to give some insight into the various ways the devil will get a foothold into our lives. Verse 28 says that the person who has been stealing should no longer yield to the temptation to steal, but should seek to work with his own hands in order to have something to share with those in need. One foothold the devil will use in this area, is that of making us feel dissatisfied with what we have, then once he has that foothold, he can easily move to the next foothold of theft.

Verse 29 then goes on to tell us that we should not let any unwholesome talk come out of our mouths, but only what is helpful for building others up according to their needs, that it may benefit those who listen. This is a very interesting foothold. What is unwholesome talk? I feel this means any talk which is unclean, smutty, or degrading to others. Once we allow anything of this nature to come on our lips, it will be a foothold that the devil can use to gain the next foothold of backbiting, gossip and the like.

We continue then with verse 30 that says we are not to grieve the Holy Spirit of God. How do we grieve the Spirit of God? By allowing our bodies to be used for things that will bring dishonour to God's name. As we have already seen, our bodies are the temples of the Holy Spirit and we should be always be alert not to allow things into our life that would grieve Him.

We come now to verse 31. The instruction here is that we are to get rid of all bitterness, rage and anger, brawling and slander, along with every form of malice. Quite a list of footholds here to beware of.

Imbalance

One of the most subtle of Satan's tactics that he seems to use especially on those who he cannot find an inroad into in any other way, is that of imbalance. In other words pushing us too far one way. One way of putting it is when someone has a favourite doctrine or teaching, and they become overbalanced on it to the extent that they will not listen to anyone who has a different opinion to them.

Balance is not just to do with pounds and ounces, weights and measures but Job equates it with integrity (Proverbs 11:1; Job 31:6).

One thing that Satan will often use in making us imbalanced is our human reasoning. Human reasoning and faith are not compatible when it comes to the things of God. Our minds will try and work everything out on a human level but the way God often works is beyond our human reasoning. When you consider many of the stories in the Bible, they are totally impractical to the human mind. Just look for a moment at the way Jericho was captured. God said to come against a heavily fortressed city with trumpets and shouting! Our human reasoning says not to be so daft, but that is the way God said it was to be done and that was the way Jericho was captured. We will either have to hold on to our human reasoning or have faith in what God has said (1 Corinthians 2:13; 1 Corinthians 9:8). We cannot have both when we are dealing with the things of the Spirit of God, for God works in the way that He desires and who are we to gainsay Him? Isaiah 55:8 and 9 tells us that God says that His thoughts and ways are not our thoughts and ways, that

His thoughts and ways are higher than ours. This is because we only reason with our human minds until we are filled with the Holy Spirit and yield ourselves to have the mind of Christ (Romans 12:2; 1 Corinthians 2:16).

So we have looked at a few of the things that Satan will use as tactics to make us ineffective in our walk with God and in our growth as children of God. There are probably many more that you could think of and Satan will always be using new ways, because every time we become aware of one of his tactics he will subtly change it.

Chapter 37

How to Handle Failure

It is hard today to find a person who has not at some time in their life faced a situation in which they had felt a failure. Failure is a part of our human condition. Often we feel that because we have failed, God will not want to use us, nor will He love us. If we do fail some of us take years to recover. Others of us are often reluctant to admit that we have failed. Still others of us feel that we are constantly failing and missing the mark.

How we handle failure will depend upon our relationship with God. When we have developed a good relationship with God then we will be able to admit freely that we have failed.

Most of us are often very quick to condemn ourselves, let alone others who fail. We do not consider the fact that some of the people in the Bible, many of those that we hold as 'heroes of faith' were also failures.

Noah – the man who God used to save His creation. What happened to him? He planted a vineyard, that was not wrong. He made some wine, and that was not wrong either, but then he drunk so much of the wine that he became drunk! (Genesis 9:20–21). Yet he is mentioned in the well-known faith chapter of the Bible (Hebrews 11:7) as one of the great men of the Old Testament. Today if someone in one of our churches got drunk, what would happen to them? Usually they would be condemned, taken out of any office they held and generally made to feel bad. But Noah was still esteemed even though he failed.

Abraham – the man God used to bring His blessing upon all nations, the man of faith, yet the man who deceived Pharaoh (Genesis 12:11–13).

Isaac – who deceived in just the same way as his father (Genesis 26:7). He is also listed in Hebrews 11.

Moses – the man God used to deliver His people from the slavery of Egypt. But he did not trust God enough the Bible tells us, and because of this he was not allowed to go into the Promised Land! (Numbers 20:11–12). He also murdered a man (Exodus 2:11–12).

Samson – he had little of a godly character, nevertheless he is listed in Hebrews as one of the great men.

King David – a man who God said was after His own heart, yet who committed adultery, then murder, to try and cover up his sin (2 Samuel 11).

Many of the Judges during the conquest of Canaan were outstanding spiritual leaders, but the truth is that today we would have been embarrassed by their actions. Many of the Old Testament kings went into idolatry, and Solomon was among them.

In the New Testament there are others for us to consider:

Peter – who denied being with Jesus.

Demas – Paul said he fell back because he loved the world (2 Timothy 4:10).

If any of these men were in our society today they would probably all be classed as failures. Yet there they are in scripture, for everyone to see, held up as God's people of faith, there for us all to read about. Failures? No, not failures, but people who God could use, following Him with as much of their heart as they could, with the grace revealed to them. They were committed to their God as much as they could be. Yes, they failed, but that did not disqualify them. For some of them, God could use them just because they had failed.

We are all human, just like these characters we have looked at. We all live with the possibility of failing. After his failure, David was deeply repentant (Psalm 51). David's qualification to succeed Saul was not his human attainment, nor his stature, nor his heritage, nor that he had achieved very high academic qualifications. No, his heart, not his perfection, was his qualification. God said of David that he was a man after His own heart! (1 Samuel 13:14). I believe this meant that his attitude was right before God. Our heart-attitude will dictate to us how we react in and to situations.

In Matthew chapter 14 we have the story of the incident when Peter walked on the water of the Sea of Galilee. Often, when this story is looked at, all we hear about is the fact that Peter sank and the Lord saved him. I want to consider the fact that, after Peter began to sink and the Lord caught him by his hand and lifted him on top of the water again, that Peter then walked back to the boat with Jesus. After his failure, the Lord lifted him up and then he succeeded! I like to think of this incident as a victory for Peter and not a failure. We can take the same principle into our lives. Once we find ourselves failing we can cry out to the Lord for help and then He can turn our failure into a success for us and a victory over circumstances that could have drowned us. The devil loves to take us into situations that mean we need the help of the Lord, but blinds us to the fact that we have the strength of the Lord, the power of the Holy Spirit, and our faith in God to rely upon. Most of us fail because we attempt to do things in our own strength. We put our faith in:

– what we know,
– what we have learnt,
– what we have been trained to do,
– what we have succeeded in before.

We do not consider what the Bible tells us in Colossians 3:17 that whatever we do (this means anything and everything, whether in word or in action), we should do it all in the name of the Lord Jesus. Then in Philippians 4:13 we have the much quoted verse when Paul claimed that he could do everything through God who gave him strength. We have the same God and the same strength available to us today. Peter tells us in 1 Peter 4:11 that whenever anyone speaks, and when anyone serves, we should do it with the strength God provides, so that in all things God may be praised through Jesus Christ.

If we can change our thinking to include God's enabling in all that we do, turning to Him for help in all we do and say, then I am sure we would soon find that our failure and success record will change drastically.

The antidote to failure is the confidence that we have already looked at in Part Two.

Chapter 38

Self-Respect

Self-respect! There are those of us who have an erroneous belief that as Christians we should not have any self-respect or any self-image. I say erroneous, because I strongly believe it is an error, or at least a misunderstanding.

Jesus told us that there were two great commandments. The first was that we were to love the Lord our God with all our heart, soul, mind and strength. The second was to love your neighbour as yourself (Mark 12:29–31). We have already looked at these verses before in other contexts. Jesus is suggesting here that if we are going to be effective in showing love to our neighbour we first have to love ourselves. This in no way means that we are selfish! Selfishness is sin! But what it does mean is that we have begun to accept who we are. We respect who God has made us. If the devil can twist love to be selfish, there must be real love because he has made nothing himself but only a forgery of what God has created.

This means accepting who we are – who God has made us – including our sexuality. The Bible is full of stories about people's sexuality whether good or bad. Sometimes a person's sexuality led them away from God into immorality. We commonly call this lust. This is a passion that takes control of our life so strongly that the intensity of our desire means we lust after it until we get it. This usually involves sexual relationships between men and women.

The assumption that sexual passion is a result of the fall rather than the good idea of our Creator, most likely goes back to the early Christian times. The Bible begins with the body in creation and ends with the body redeemed from sin and raised in resurrection power.

The whole story of creation is a body becoming alive to God. When God breathed life into Adam he became a living soul. The body was created first, the soul and spirit came after. We were created body first and we must come to the place of acceptance of our body, its sexual desires and responses. Sexual drive is not sin. Uncontrolled sexual drive leads us into sin. Sexuality as part of God's image, is what drives us towards intimacy with people. We need to have a total acceptance of who God has made us and a total acceptance of who we are.

If you do not have an acceptance of yourself you will not be able to give yourself to others. There is no time to waste on self-pity, bewailing your status, or constantly longing to be something you are not. If you live in this state it means you have become a victim. Being a victor will mean accepting yourself. Accepting who you are and having a relationship with God. This will mean that you are not constantly asking God for solutions to what you see are problems, but relating to Him from a state of victory.

Within each of us is the femininity that God created us with and we need to accept that. For some it will mean dealing with a desire to have been born male. When we truly accept who God has made us we will develop a strength of character which will enable us to make the right decisions and not compromise, going after God with all your heart in order to be the woman God wants you to be.

All that is left for you to do is accept the victory that has been accomplished upon the Cross by Jesus Christ, making it a reality in your life and then living victoriously. Not under the circumstance but under the Lord Jesus Christ.

If we do not learn to take ourselves seriously and accept ourselves as we are, we cannot expect others to accept us and take us seriously. If there is no acceptance of ourselves, and no belief in who God has made us then will there will be a lack of self-worth. A lack of self-worth can lead to guilt. We will feel guilty because we are not a whole person. This can lead us into becoming introverted, which in turn leads many to look for reasons why they are like they are. They may believe that something that happened in the past, either in childhood or even to their ancestors, has resulted in them being the way they are.

You are a new creature in Christ, old things have passed away, all things have become new (2 Corinthians 5:17). Begin to believe it and walk in it. Begin to believe what God says about being new, begin to be fulfilled as a woman.

All of us as human beings have a need to be needed. Don't think about having a need to be filled but think about fulfilling a need in someone else. God created us with a need to belong. God said that it was not good for Adam to be alone so He made him a helper – Eve. Don't think that fulfilment only comes in being joined to a partner in marriage. Outside of marriage, we all still need to be fulfilled.

Someone once said that 'We can live a full life even when we haven't got everything we want.' Living life to the full and finding fulfilment, is not in what we possess in material goods, but what we have in our walk with God, in our spiritual life. Many married women have unfulfilled desires, they live a life feeling totally unfulfilled. Fulfilment comes from your inner being. It comes from what is inside, not from an outward status. God made us to find fulfilment in Him, not in anything or anyone else. If we do not find fulfilment in our relationship with God then we certainly will find no fulfilment outside of that.

We need to face up to the challenge of living a fulfilled

life in spite of your unfulfilled desires. Most of us will find fulfilment in knowing that God has something for us to do. In other words we must find out the gift and call of God upon our lives. No, it is not just the people that are preachers or ministers, pastors, missionaries etc. that need a call from God. I believe each one of us as a Christian needs to know our call. To put it another way, we all need to know our place in the Body of Christ. That call may or may not be to full-time ministry but we all need to know what purpose God has for our life.

This may or may not include our talents, our natural abilities. Because we enjoy doing something it does not mean that that is our gift, nor does it mean that God will not want to use us in that realm. I have met many people who have felt that because they enjoyed doing something, that God could not possibly call them to do that. They believe that God only calls people to do things that they will find hard and difficult to do. Rubbish! I cannot remember the last time I did something that I did not fully enjoy doing. Some women have said to me 'But I don't have any gifts! God has not given me talents!' or 'I was missing when God dished out gifts to people!' Again – Rubbish! God has created us in His own image. One thing God is, is a creator. Therefore within each one of us is the ability to create something! All we have to do is to discover what that is. Find out for yourself what it is that God has given you as a natural talent, then begin to use that for His glory. If you don't know what that talent is, ask your family, your friends, those closest to you. You will soon discover that there are things in your life that others recognise that you have not seen. Begin by being a good steward of what God has already given you before you start to ask Him for more. In Matthew 25:24–29 we have the well known parable of the talents, it concludes with verse 29:

> 'For everyone who has will be given more, and he will have an abundance. Whoever does not have, even what he has will be taken from him.'

Start by valuing what God has given you, do not belittle those gifts but develop them, perfect them, mature them, so that you become skilled at them.

God's desire for us is to grow and mature. First of all to grow in what He has already given to us. God accepts us as we are, true, but He does not expect us to stay there (Ephesians 4:13; Hebrews 5:14; James 1:4). God's desire is to free us from all the hurt, bondage and rejections that have come into our lives. He also wants to free us from inferiority and bring us into freedom to be who He has made us to be. So often we put limitations upon ourselves, limitations that God has not placed there.

When we begin to start to know who we are, then we can come to the point of accepting ourselves. This will result in self-worth, and self-respect. It is a fact of life that we have to live with ourselves and if we are constantly living with an attitude of failure, always belittling ourselves we will eventually not respect ourselves.

I can hear many of you asking how you equate this with humility. Humility is not in belittling yourself, it is in forgetting about yourself. Considering your brother or sister in Christ before considering yourself.

Self-respect is not making yourself out to be someone special, it is just accepting yourself.

You are God's temple. God lives within you. There are numerous scriptures that give us this truth (1 Corinthians 6:19; 1 Corinthians 3:16; 2 Corinthians 6:16). We house the Holy Spirit as well as our heart, will, mind and emotions. The Holy Spirit is as a guest within us. Whenever a guest comes to live in our home there is one thing for sure and that is that all who live in the house know that there is a guest. There is evidence that the guest is in residence. In most homes whenever a guest is coming the house is swept and tidied, and it is kept that way the whole time they are there. There can be other things which the parents ask of any child out of respect for the guest. I believe it should be the same in our lives when the Holy Spirit is present. There should be evidence that He dwells within us. The way we conduct our lives, the language we use, the conversation pieces, making room for our guest to live, can all be evidence of a house guest.

I did not choose the type of 'house' I have, that was given to me at birth, but I can choose how I utilise my house. I can make a choice of what I allow into my house. Whatever attitude I have, I do it as a choice of my will. If I choose to be humble it is a matter of my will, it is my choice.

If there is something about your external appearance which you do not like there is not much you can do about it, but you can choose how you dress yourself, how you present yourself, and what your character is.

If you cannot respect yourself then what you are really saying is that God did not know what He was doing when he sent Jesus to die on the cross in order to redeem you, because you were not worth redeeming.

Begin to respect yourself and use what God has given you. God made each one of us with gifts. Discover what they are and use them. There may be some of you who feel that as young people you were never given the opportunity to use and discover your gifts. Do not let that stop you, begin now to find out what they are. No matter what age you are, God can still make something out of your life. You will never discover your gifts if you say 'I can't'. Those words should never be heard from the mouth of a Christian. Don't place limitations upon yourself that God has not placed there.

To respect yourself is not a boosting of your ego, nor a blowing of your own trumpet but it is a recognition of who you are in Christ. Respecting what God has made you and what He has placed within you, His temple. Therefore we need to respect ourselves and look after the temple of the Holy Spirit. This is not an outward show of *'haute couture'*, of keeping to all the top fashions. What it does mean is that we dress as becomes a godly woman. In 1 Timothy 2:9 Paul gives us his thoughts on how we should dress. He says it should be modestly, with decency and propriety, not with braided hair or gold or pearls or expensive clothes, appropriate for women who profess to worship God. I feel this means that we should be clean in our appearance. We should not dress in clothes which would draw attention to us. Not relying upon expensive clothes, jewellery and other adornments to gain the attention and approval of others. We should have confidence in who we are in God. Respecting ourselves as people who the Holy Spirit dwells in, our appearance should say something about us.

I have written about the quiet spirit spoken of in 1 Peter 3:4 in a previous section but now I want to look at the statement before that, which tells us that the beauty we have should be that of your inner self, the unfading beauty of a gentle and quiet spirit, which is of great worth in God's sight. A spirit that is right with God will outshine all the fashionable clothes, make-up, hair-do's, jewellery, etc.

There are two stories in the Bible which I find very interesting. One is in Daniel 1:8–16 where we have the account of Daniel and his three friends who we are told did not want to defile themselves with food that as Hebrews they were not permitted to eat, because it did not comply with their health laws. They were give ten days to prove themselves, after which, because they looked so well, the rest of the king's men were put on the same food. I believe that this teaches us that when we live our lives in accordance with God's ways, then we have no need to fear that we will not be as good as others in the world. In fact we have to accept the fact that Daniel and his three friends were in reality better than those who had the other food. Obeying God will never be a disadvantage to us. No matter what area we apply this principle to, it will work for our benefit.

Then in the story of Esther, we read that she had six months of preparations with cosmetics before she was presented to the king. I am not sure how some modern day Christians would react if they were told that in order to be able to fulfil God's plan for their life they had to go to a beauty farm for six months! It is not wrong to use cosmetics, but I do believe it is wrong to spend money which we need to keep a roof over our heads, food in our stomachs, and clothes on our backs, on cosmetics which are very expensive.

Paul tells us to let our moderation be known in all things. I like to apply this to us as women in the area of our clothes and cosmetics. It also applies to every other area of our life. Moderation means not excessive, not OTT (Over The Top) as we may say.

I believe self-respect will come out of our relationship with God. We will also need to balance this with what we have looked at in our last section on humility and not think too highly of ourselves.

I can hear some of you saying, just a moment; what about what Jesus teaches us from Luke 14:26, Matthew 16:24 and John 12:25, where He implies that we must hate our family, lose our life and deny ourselves, and only when we have done these things can we truly be His followers? Here is the difference between selfishness and selflessness. Selfishness is loving ourselves, selflessness is denying ourselves and loving others. It is the difference between always doing what we want or denying ourselves and doing what we know God wants us to do.

If we obey the injunction of Romans 15:7 when Paul tells us to accept one another, just as Christ accepted you, we will need to start by accepting ourselves and respecting ourselves. We will never be able to truly accept others unless we have accepted ourselves.

One thing which very often stops us from accepting ourselves is when we compare ourselves with others. Because we consider we do not to come up to the standard of others, we feel we cannot accept ourselves. Maybe you compare yourself with your mother, sister, peers, friends, church members, or others. But each one of us is unique. You can never be like anyone else, so you have lost before you begin, if you go down that road. God has given you gifts that are yours and therefore you do not need to compare yourself with anyone else.

In the early years of our ministry many people who knew my parents would often compare me with my mother. Unknown to them this caused me great problems. I wanted to be known for who I was, not because of who my mother was. I was looking for my own identity in Christ. While people were comparing me with my mother I was unable to find my own identity, my own walk with God and my own spiritual standard. It was not until I came free from this that I was able to begin to find out for myself what gifts God had given me. In the same way people were also expecting me to be like my husband. Those of you who know Don know that God has called him and greatly anointed him with the ministry of evangelism. Somehow it does not matter what subject Don preaches on, people always come to know Jesus as a result. I believe this is because the anointing of evangelism is upon him. My gift is different. Evangelism is not my talent. For years I tried hard to live up to my husband's gift. It was not until I relaxed and allowed God to give me His gift for my life that I was free to develop that gift.

Comparing ourselves with others will stop us from developing the gift that God has for us. In Galatians 6:4–5 we read that each one must test his own actions, and take a pride in himself without comparison to anyone else, for each should carry his own load. This is a stepping stone to accepting who you are.

Involved with 'not comparing' ourselves with others is the whole idea of competition, or living up to someone else's expectations of us. We are not in a contest to see who can win, or who is the fittest, or who has the most stamina. We are like some of the people who enter a marathon; just there to complete the course, not to see how fast we can do it. In view of this we use self-respect, accepting our abilities and not going beyond ourselves. In 2 Corinthians 10:13 Paul tells us that we should not *'boast beyond proper limits, but will confine our boasting to the field God has assigned to us.'* In the same way we should not brag and boast about our walk with God, nor our own gifts and abilities, but respect who God has made us with the gifts He has given us. Paul tells us in Romans 12:3 that we should not think of ourselves more highly than we ought, but rather think of ourselves with realistic judgment.

Living in victory will mean that we have begun to respect ourselves. Satan will try to do all in his power to keep us ineffective and weak as a Christian. One way is by telling us that we are a nobody. Do not believe his lies. Instead believe what God has said about you, and live in the victory as a son of God.

Chapter 39

Living Positively

Our thought life can be our biggest enemy as we seek to have a victorious life.

Dr Kate Smith (a doctor of psychiatry) has stated that it is your attitude that determines the quality of your life, not your health.

We are told in the scriptures that our body is the temple of the Holy Spirit (1 Corinthians 6:19; 1 Corinthians 3:16; 2 Corinthians 6:16). I have made numerous references to this throughout the book already. I now want to look it from another angle.

What I put into my 'house' is my choice. If I thank God for my body and as an act of my will decide to offer it to God as a Holy Sacrifice it is for me, and only me to decide. It is my choice if I have a positive attitude or not. Only I can decide how I use my 'house' and what I put into it. When I became a Christian it was a choice I made, an act of my will. Then when I was filled with the Holy Spirit, I had to yield my life to the Lord. It was a matter of my choice. I still then have to make the choice to allow the Spirit of God to flow through me or not. It is the Life of God that should be manifested on the outside but so often it is not. It is my mind, my will, my emotions that are seen by others. The choice is mine. I have the choice to let Satan and the world to tell me how to think and what to believe or I can choose to let the Word of God lead me into all truth and into victory.

In this context I want to look at three areas. Each area will mean that we will have to make a choice about it, they are:

(a)   a positive outlook
(b)   a sense of humour
(c)   our attitude.

A positive outlook begins in our minds. In Part Two we looked at the character of a godly woman and mentioned 1 Corinthians 13. There is one verse in that chapter which often seems to be missed or overlooked, either because we wish it was not there, or because we do not like what it says, for it means we have to do something about it.

In 1 Corinthians 13:11 Paul said that when he was a child he talked, thought and reasoned like a child, but when he became a man, he put away childish things. How does a child talk? Often by using the words me, my, mine. How does a child think? It goes by what it sees; it does not go any deeper. If a child observes a car driving down the road it only considers the wheels and the body work, it has no understanding of the engine with its pistons, gear-box, oil, water, petrol etc. It only considers what it can see with its eyes. It does not consider what it cannot see. How does a child reason if something is fair or unfair? 'She has more sweets than I have.' 'She is allowed to stay out longer than I am.'

When we become mature we are told by Paul that we should put this kind of behaviour and thinking behind us. The problem for many of us is that we are still thinking, talking and reasoning like children. We have not matured to become adults in our thinking and thought life. Since becoming a Christian we have carried the same childish behaviour over into our spiritual life and walk with God. We see someone else getting blessed and we say – 'God it's not fair.' We see things from the external and we never begin to try and see things from the internal, the way God sees things. We talk like children, always thinking of what is in it for me and not really thinking about others.

I want us to look at how people in the Bible thought, and the results of those thoughts. In 1 Samuel 1 we have the story of the birth of Samuel. It begins with Hannah at the temple praying. We are told that she was praying in her heart, her lips were moving, but her voice was not heard. We are then told that Eli thought she was drunk. Hannah was misunderstood by Eli. He 'thought' she was drunk when in fact she was communicating with God.

In 1 Samuel 16 we read how the prophet Samuel arrives at the home of Jesse where God has instructed him to go in order to anoint the next king of Israel. When he saw Eliab he thought, 'Surely the Lord's anointed stands here before the LORD.' Samuel 'thought' that the eldest would be the one God chose to be king, but we all now know that his thoughts were wrong. It was the youngest of Jesse's children that God had chosen to be king.

In 2 Kings 5 we read of Naaman the leper who had come to the prophet to be healed. We are told that Naaman went away angry and said,

> *'I thought that he would surely come out to me and stand and call on the name of the LORD his God, wave his hand over the spot and cure me of my leprosy.'*

Naaman 'thought' about how God was going to heal him. Many of us today have thoughts and ideas on how God is going to work for us, or how He is going to heal us, or another person.

Looking further into scripture we can discover many other things about men's thoughts. In Genesis 6:5 we read that the LORD saw how great man's wickedness on the earth had become, and that every inclination of the thoughts of his heart was only evil all the time. Here is an inference that wickedness had become so great in the earth because of man's thought life.

When we continue to live from our human spirit we will

soon become a victim of our thoughts. In 1 Chronicles 28:9 we read that the LORD searches every heart and understands every motive behind the thoughts. Even when we think we are right so often we are not because the motivation behind our thoughts are not pure. Although we put on a good show to those around us, trying to make them believe that our thoughts are pure when in reality they are not. It will do us no good because God sees the motivation behind our thoughts.

It is also very interesting that the Bible tells us that our thoughts are futile (Psalm 94:11). Many of our thoughts come from anxiety (Psalm 139:23). God has a lot to say about worry.

God knows our thoughts and our reasoning. Sometimes we are not sure ourselves about why we think the way we do but God knows every motive. Most of our thoughts cause us to worry over situations. David the Psalmist said Psalm 13:2:

> *'How long must I wrestle with my thoughts and every day have sorrow in my heart? How long will my enemy triumph over me?'*

It would appear that he had a battle with his own thoughts which brought him sorrow of heart.

God wants us to see things His way and not our human way. He desires us to go beyond our human spirits into His Spirit (Isaiah 55:8–9). God's thoughts penetrate into the heart of the situation and not just on the surface as our human thoughts so easily do. We have to become adult in our thinking and put way those childish thoughts, as we saw earlier. Only then we will start to think as God wants us to think.

One of the ways to begin thinking in the way God wants, is to do what we are told in Hebrews 3:1; to fix our thoughts on Jesus. This does not mean that we walk around with our heads in the clouds but it does mean that we become like Jesus and our thought life comes in line with the Word of God. Proverbs 23:7 says as a man thinks in his heart that is what he will become. You may have been told negative things about yourself, things like – 'You are no good,' or 'You will never become anything.' Maybe you overheard people talking negatively about you; it may have been your parents, your brothers and sisters, a teacher, or a friend. Those words have become seeds in your mind that you have begun to believe are the truth, so now you think negatively about yourself. If this continues long enough those thoughts will so take hold of you that they actually become a reality in your life.

2 Corinthians 10:5 instructs us to take every thought captive, in order to make it obedient to Christ. It is something which we have to do. We, ourselves, have to take **every** thought captive. Not just those we want to but every thought. That means the thoughts that are contrary to what we know is according to the Word of God. When we can make every thought obedient to Christ then the negatives will soon become positives because God only has positive thoughts about us.

We must then go a little further and consider what Paul tells us in Colossians 3:1–2:

> *'Since, then, you have been raised with Christ, set your hearts on things above, where Christ is seated at the right hand of God. Set your minds on things above, not on earthly things.'*

In these two verses we have two different things to look at; the first – that we have to set our hearts on things above. This lines up with the teaching of Jesus in Matthew 6:21, where He tells us that where our treasure is, there our heart will be also. Our hearts should be set on the things of God, and specifically around the throne of God, for that is where Jesus is seated – at the right hand of God!

It is easy for us to set our hearts on things of this earth because those are the things that concern us at this point in time. Our family, our survival – whether it is financially, economically, or business wise – our career prospects, and yes, even church. These are all very legitimate things but the important thing is where we set our hearts. Where are our goals? What are we aiming for – a prosperous life down here or rewards in heaven?

This then brings us to the second point; that we need to set our minds on things above. Our mind, it has been stated, is a battleground for the devil. Whatever takes our thoughts or our pre-occupation will determine our goals. In order for us to develop a Christ-like life (and behaviour) there must be a preoccupation with 'things above'. These things are a conscious worship of God's character. What we worship is what we become like.

Some people ponder and brood over their past victories and failures and they then live in the past. Their days begin with the past, therefore they are not really in what they are doing today.

Positions, possessions, and pleasure are all the same. When they are things which control our thoughts they will become what we worship. Learning to worship is the key to mind control and character development. We need to ask ourself – 'What do we set our thoughts on?' Only you can answer that question. Whatever your answer is, that is what you will become like. If you do not like your answer, or you do not think that your answer is according to what we see in scripture then you can change. God tells us that character can be changed. We can allow His Spirit to transform us. It is not just left for events to control. We can change by setting our minds upon the things we are told in scripture.

In Romans 12:1–2 we have a definite link between worship and the way we think. It says that when we offer our bodies up as living sacrifices – and that means surrendering our will to His will – we are actually performing an act of worship to God. The next step for us is the changing of our mind set. There must be the possibility for us to renew our minds through God's power or else Paul would not have given us this instruction.

It is also interesting to note that he puts the ball firmly into our court – he says *'do not'*, it is an action. *'The pattern of this world'*, means that the world will teach us things that are contrary to the Word of God. We therefore have to put some effort into the transforming of our minds. The world's way of thinking is opposed to God's way of thinking. Until our minds have been transformed, we will never be able to find out what God's will is. Let me assure you that this is not an easy thing, it is something that we will have to work hard at.

In Romans 8:5–9 Paul says the *'mind of the sinful man.'* Another way of putting this is the carnal man. The person who is not really spiritual sets his mind upon the things that are not of God, and that leads to death. The mind that is being controlled by the Spirit of God has life and peace. The sinful mind is hostile towards God because it does not submit to God's law, in fact it cannot do so; only the mind controlled by His Spirit can be in harmony, submissive and obedient to Christ. Until we have had our minds transformed, we cannot totally submit to God's law.

Our natural minds will be filled with natural desires, but when we have our minds set on what the Lord desires then we have spiritual desires. The difference is all to do with our minds. When we know the Lord, then there is the possibility of our minds being transformed.

You may think that this is something that we will never attain to, that it is beyond our reach. In our wildest dreams we think it would be absolutely wonderful to be able to think as the Spirit of God wants us to think. What does Paul tell us in 1 Corinthians 2:16? He tells us that we have the mind of Christ! How positive Paul is here. He says it as a statement of fact. We actually have the mind of Christ. Many of us would react by saying that we do not have the mind of Christ. If we are going to believe the scriptures then we have to begin to believe that we do have the mind of Christ. Once we have totally surrendered to Him it comes within our reach.

There is another important aspect that we need to consider and that is in the area of how we think about ourselves. 2 Corinthians 5:16 tells us that we should not regard any one from a worldly point of view. Though we once regarded Christ in this way, we do so no longer. We can apply this scripture to ourselves. Do not regard or think of ourselves from a worldly point of view. How we think about ourselves will determine whether or not we have a positive attitude.

In the same way **what** we think about will determine whether we have a positive attitude or not. Paul in Philippians 4:8 gives us some very potent guidelines concerning the things we should think about. He tells us:

> *'Finally, brothers, whatever is true, whatever is noble, whatever is right, whatever is pure, whatever is lovely, whatever is admirable – if anything is excellent or praiseworthy – think about such things.'*

Quite a list, wouldn't you say? Things that are **true**, **noble** (virtuous), **right**, **pure**, **lovely**, **admirable**, **excellent**, or **praiseworthy**, these are the things we should have in our thoughts. It would be a good discipline that whenever we find ourselves thinking about things that do not come into the scope of the above we consciously stop and find something within their range to think about.

So we can conclude that to have a positive outlook means:

- That we are no longer acting like children; we have grown up.
- That we know our position in Christ.
- That we have our hearts and minds set on things above.
- That our thoughts are about things which are excellent and praiseworthy.

I read in an American magazine a while ago the following statement:

'Scientific evidence is mounting that a positive outlook and a sense of humour can bolster the immune system and enhance your health.'

When I read this I immediately thought, 'here we go again, the scientific world is proving that the Bible is right after all.' Proverbs 17:22 says that a cheerful heart is good medicine. Proverbs 15:13 also says that a happy heart makes the face cheerful. Happiness and cheerfulness will come from the characteristic we looked at in the second section – Joy. When we have this foundation of the Kingdom of God in our lives then it will naturally follow that we will have a cheerful disposition. For one cannot really have the joy of the Lord unless it affects your whole being.

A good medicine! I can remember some years ago that Don had to visit our family doctor. Before the doctor came to the point that Don had gone to see him about, he did his usual thing and asked after the whole family and about our work and ministry. In the end he said to Don – 'Mr Double, I am convinced that you can do more for 50 percent of people who come into my surgery than I can.' Meaning if only people could begin to have something to believe in, most of their illnesses could be dealt with. Most people today have nothing to believe in and live in a vacuum. Once we begin to have faith in God and receive what He has provided for us then we can live a life that is free from tension and stress. Cheerfulness is one of those keys.

The verses we read in Proverbs spoke of a crushed spirit and a heartache, both of which dry the bones and crush the spirit. Many illnesses today can be traced back to heartache, hurts and rejections caused in people's lives by unforgiveness. When we have a sense of humour and can laugh at ourselves, then we will begin to relax and enjoy life. I am sure we will soon find that many of the stresses have gone.

I have already mentioned some scriptures that speak of the joy that we can receive through our relationship with

God. Here I want to bring you just one more that I feel is a key to us living a life that is full of happiness and cheerfulness.

'No one will take away your joy.' (John 16:22)

Jesus spoke these words to His disciples when He told them that He would be going away from them. He was sure that they would grieve but He was also sure that He would see them again and then it would be impossible for any man to take away their joy. I find it interesting that Jesus said that no man would take away their joy. Once we have received and experienced the joy that should be ours through Jesus Christ then no man will be able to take it from us because it is a gift from God. I am sure some of you will be very unsure of the reality of this, because you are living a life that is joyless because of your situation, and you consider that another person is responsible for the situation.

One year at our family summer camps I took a seminar on the subject of the 'Joy of the Lord'. At the end I opened the meeting for a question and answer time. One lady asked the question if I thought it was possible to have joy in the midst of tribulation, say perhaps lying in a hospital bed. Wanting to be very positive I gave an affirmative reply. Little did I know what would happen. Up till that time I had only been in hospital twice in my life. Once when I was very young, so young that I have no real memories of it, and the second time when I had my last child (the others were all born at home). Obviously that was a very joyous time, and I was only in for 48 hours. Within an hour of returning home from that particular summer camp I found myself in hospital! I was not even allowed to put my feet over the end of the bed, and I was not allowed to have a bath. After camping for a whole month there was only one thing I wanted to do and that was to have a good soak in the bath! I can remember very clearly, at about mid-night, with the noise of a nurse's party in the ward beneath me, I began to laugh! God took my thoughts back to what I had said to this lady only two days before. Here I was now in hospital, flat on my back, with suspected thrombosis. The joy I felt in my heart and spirit was immeasurable. I chuckled to God and myself. The joy was there alright. It was true, nothing can take the joy away which is ours by right as a child of God. I need to tell you the end of the story – just before I left home Don and my family had prayed for me. The next morning at about 8 am the doctor came round to check up on me. He did a whole series of tests and said that all the symptoms that had been in my body the previous evening were gone and I could go home! Not only do we need a sense of humour but I believe God has a sense of humour. When we put ourselves out on a limb in faith, nailing our colours to the mast, we can be sure that we will be put to the test to see if it is true for us.

The abundant life that God has promised us is relevant to every aspect of our lives. When we can nurture a cheerfulness that stems from the joy which is ours because of the cross, then it will affect us and those around us.

Proverbs 15:15 says that:

'. . . the cheerful heart has a continual feast.'

We will never go without when we are cheerful because we will always have something to draw upon, and we will not be the type of person to be downcast and dejected because of circumstances. Paul tells us in the book of Philippians 4:11 that he had learned to be content whatever the circumstances. When we are cheerful then the circumstances will not affect our contentment. This is closely aligned to our next subject – that of our attitude.

I have probably already dealt with one of the subjects most people have an attitude problem with, and that is work. The older I get the more I realise that many of us pick up attitudes from those we live with more than anything else. Attitudes are always picked up, they are never taught by words alone.

Attitude means: opinion, perspective, outlook, viewpoint, stance. In other words, how we look at things; from what perspective or angle we view things. If we look at things from a human perspective we will get the wrong view of it, but when we view it from God's angle, which is how Jesus looked at things, we will then get the true perspective.

One thing scripture makes clear is that we need to be made new in the area of our attitude. It also implies that our attitude comes from our mind set. Once we have become new creations and we have put on the new self that has been created to be like God, then our minds will take on the new attitudes to go along with the new creation (Ephesians 4:22–24). The problem with most of us is that we have not yet 'put off' the old self. We are still living with the old desires and attitudes, many of which have been taught us by the world in which we live, by those we rub shoulders with daily, and by our families. If these are ungodly and worldly influences we will then have problems when it comes to the things of the Spirit and the attitudes that we should have as children of God. The Bible is adamant when it says that our attitude should be the same as that of Christ Jesus (Philippians 2:5). What was that attitude? We are told that in the next few verses of Philippians 2:6–7:

> *'Who, being in very nature God, did not consider equality with God something to be grasped, but made himself nothing, taking the very nature of a servant, being made in human likeness.'*

Jesus' attitude was that although He was in fact God, being the very Son of God, yet at the same time He did not think about equality. He lowered Himself to become a servant and took upon Himself the very nature of mankind. His attitude was one of servanthood. We saw this earlier in the instance when He washed His disciple's feet.

Jesus' attitude was that He desired to do His Fathers' will not His own. We see this when He was in the garden before He was nailed to the cross (Mark 14:36). Praying to His Father He said:

> *'Take this cup from me. Yet not what I will, but what you will.'*

If our attitude is to be the same as that of Jesus, we must come to the place where we are also willing to take whatever God's will is for us. This will mean that even when things do not seem to make sense to us, we will be like Jesus and say *'not my will but yours be done.'* This was the attitude of Jesus to surrender His life to do the will of His Father.

We also read this again in 1 Peter 4:1:

> *'Therefore, since Christ suffered in his body, arm yourselves also with the same attitude, because he who has suffered in his body is done with sin.'*

Even though doing God's will meant suffering, Jesus still had the attitude of willingness.

The question we need to ask ourselves is – do I have the kind of attitude that even if it means that I will suffer hardship, I am willing for God to have His way in my life?

Chapter 40

The Words We Speak

An area that many of us, if not all of us, have a problem with, is in the realm of our tongues. James 1:26 says that,

> 'if anyone considers himself religious and does not keep a tight rein on his tongue, he deceives himself and his religion is worthless.'

When we consider ourselves children of God then this verse is being addressed to us. We need to 'keep a tight rein' on the words we speak. This theme is carried through in James 3. We so easily find a way in which to control animals and in particular a horse, which is so much bigger than us. Yet we fail to be able to find a way to bring our own tongues under control. In the same way we have devised a way in which to control a ship, which again is larger than us, and that device is very small in comparison with the size of the ship. Even though we have been able to use our knowledge to invent these devices we have not used that same knowledge to control our own tongue which is such a small member of our own bodies.

James goes on with another illustration – that of a fire that consumes a whole forest of trees. One little spark ignites a fire that spreads so quickly that it can destroy a vast forest. He says that this is the way in which our tongue can defile our own body, which in turn corrupts our relationship with God and with men.

We boast great achievements in the scientific world, engineering world, medical world, and manufacturing world, yet we still fail to tame and control our tongue. Just when we think we have achieved a victory it goes and lets us down again! We have a tremendous time at church, praising and worshipping God. We come out feeling on top of the world, ready to take on anything and anyone, then we discover someone has reversed into our new car and dented it. As the saying goes, 'the air turns blue!' Or we arrive home to find that the lunch has been burnt to a cinder. How quickly the nice feelings of church disappear under a cloud of words that we have held in check for so long. All our hard work with the discipline of our tongue has gone in one moment. James says that these things ought not to be. But how can we help it, we cry? 'It always seems to be there rearing its ugly head. What can I do to stop these sudden outbursts?'

The Psalmist gives us a good insight when he prays that the words of his mouth and the meditation of his heart might be pleasing to God (Psalm 19:14). One of the first things we must do is go to God in prayer, desperate and humble, asking for the Holy Spirit to come and empower us to control our tongue. We can then begin to do some practical exercises and stop using some of the words we do, in the way we do.

For example, in Matthew 5:22 Jesus tells us that anyone who says, *'You fool'* will be in danger of the fire of hell. Yet so often we quickly deride and debase our fellow man, be it a child, our spouse, our close friend. Often we say that it is only done in fun, but when we consider the Word of God that is not so. How often do we hear adults calling children names, such as monkeys, kids, brats etc., then wonder why in a little while their behaviour begins to resemble that of the name we have called them! Proverbs 6:2 tells us that we are ensnared by the words of our mouths. What we speak will quickly bring us into bondage. We must also realise that words we speak will affect the lives of other people, especially when they are words of criticism. To be ensnared means that we are trapped. Often we say things so quickly that we don't think through what we say, and then we have the unenviable situation where we have to renege on what we have uttered.

Paul tells us in Ephesians 4:29 that we should not let any unwholesome talk come out of our mouths, but only what is helpful for building others up according to their needs, that it may benefit those who listen. I believe that unwholesome talk means anything that is degrading to another person, or anything that will cause a bad seed to be sown in a person's heart that later could develop into a big issue in their life.

Proverbs 12:18 tells us that,

> *'Reckless words pierce like a sword, but the tongue of the wise brings healing.'*

I have been in many situations where words have been spoken that have caused hurt, and it has been a very long time before there has been healing from those words. We have already looked at the issue of wisdom for us as children of God and this is one area in particular that we need much wisdom so that our words will not cause hurt to others.

There are many more scriptures for us to look at; too many for us to comment on here. When we read Proverbs 16:21; Psalm 34:13; Proverbs 10:19; Proverbs 15:4; Psalm 114:3; Proverbs 4:24; Matthew 12:34, there are a few things for us to take note of:

- Our words can be either a blessing or be destructive. They can be used to bring healing, or they can be used to crush others.
- We can ask God for His help in controlling our tongue.

- We have to do something towards controlling the words we speak. We are told to 'put away', to hold our tongue, and to keep our tongue, they are all things that we can do to help.
- The words we do speak will come from what is in our hearts.

In the light of this we understand that if we desire to control our tongue and the words we speak, we need to pay attention to what is going into our hearts. When we consider the last three things we looked at, a positive outlook on life, a sense of humour, and our attitudes, and weigh them against what we have just been looking at in the area of the words we speak, then we can see that all of them are closely linked to living a victorious life as a child of God.

Chapter 41

Grace to Live By

Grace is a subject that we can never seem to get to the bottom of. It has been said that it is something for nothing for those who did not deserve anything. While I would agree with this, I feel that it is only half a picture of what grace is.

Grace appears to me to have two dimensions in the New Testament. There is the aspect that we hear most about, that of the grace of God that came to us when Jesus died for our salvation, and it is something that God has towards us. I am in total agreement with this. But while studying the subject some years ago I discovered another aspect of God's grace.

I do not ever think we will be able to express in our language what God's grace is because it is deeper than we will ever be able to fathom. My computer Bible tells me that the word 'grace' appears a total of 131 times.

Beginning in the Old Testament we discover that grace is something that God gives to those who are humble (Proverbs 3:34). This means that His grace was available before the cross of Jesus Christ. It is a gift that is given by God to man. When someone gives you a gift it actually belongs to you. They do not come along the next day and take it away. If they did, the gift would no longer be yours. In the same way any gift that the Word of God says God gives to us, is ours. He does not suddenly take it away. So when we are told that God gives grace to the humble it is something that the humble person receives to help them have humility. It is tangible.

In the New Testament we are told that as a child Jesus grew and the grace of God was upon Him (Luke 2:40). From this I deduce that grace is something that is very practical, it is something that will help us to grow and mature. We are then told in Acts 4:33 that,

> *'With great power the apostles continued to testify to the resurrection of the Lord Jesus, and much grace was upon them all.'*

Notice it says *'upon them'*, again an indication that it is something tangible. Not just something that God has towards us but something that He has bestowed upon us. Again in Acts 6:8 we understand that when Stephen started to operate in his gift as a deacon in the New Testament Church, one of the things that stood out about him was the fact that he was *'full of God's grace.'* Because of it he did great wonders and miraculous signs among the people. Once more we see the aspect of grace being something that is practical in helping Stephen to perform his ministry. Still in the book of Acts turn to 11:23 and we read that when Barnabas arrived at Antioch he was able to see the evidence of the grace of God in the Christian's lives. It was able to be seen, visible.

Paul tells us many times that the grace of God has either been given to us, or that God gave him grace (Romans 15:15; 1 Corinthians 1:4; Ephesians 3:7, 8; Ephesians 4:7; 1 Corinthians 3:10; 1 Timothy 1:14). Again we see it as a gift that God has given in order to help us. Paul says in 1 Corinthians 15:10 that it is only by the grace of God that he was what he was, and that the grace given to him was not without effect. In fact it enabled him to work harder than all of them. In 2 Corinthians 9:8 Paul instructs us that,

*'God is able to make **all** grace abound to you, so that in **all** things at **all** times, having **all** that you need, you will abound in every good work.'*

This is a key verse because it tells us that the grace of God will help us in **all things**, at **all times**, and that it will give us **all** *that we need in order for us to do* **all** *that is necessary.*

Have you ever been in a situation that you have found hard? You felt that it would be impossible for you to handle and cope with, and you were out of your depth? That is when you needed the grace of God. Paul writes in 2 Corinthians 9:14 that it was because of the surpassing grace of God that was given to them, that they were able to witness and give as generously as they did. Then while Paul was writing about all the trials and persecutions that he went through, he makes an amazing statement. He says that God told him that,

'My grace is sufficient for you, for my power is made perfect in weakness.'   (2 Corinthians 12:9)

Therefore Paul says he will boast all the more gladly about his weaknesses, so that Christ's power may rest upon him. It was the grace of God given to Paul during his persecutions that enabled him to endure. Today there are many Christians around the world who are able to testify to the same grace given to them, enabling them to endure persecutions also. When we feel weak and unable to stand up under the persecution it is then that we need the grace of God to endure. We do not need it when everything is going nice and easy.

We then come to another area which Paul applies the gift of grace to, and this is found in Colossians 4:6. He tells us that our conversation should always be full of grace, seasoned with salt, so that we may know how to answer everyone. This goes back to what I said in the last section, about the words we speak. In order to correct the way we speak we need to apply the grace of God to our lips.

> *'For the grace of God that brings salvation has appeared to all men. It teaches us to say "No" to ungodliness and worldly passions, and to live self-controlled, upright and godly lives in this present age.'*
>
> (Titus 2:11, 12)

Here it would appear that the grace of God helps us to live our lives as God desires, in holiness. This is repeated in 1 Peter 1:13:

> *'Therefore, prepare your minds for action; be self-controlled; set your hope fully on the grace to be given you when Jesus Christ is revealed.'*

In order to prepare our minds for action and to use self-control it would appear that we need the grace of God.

I believe that we need the grace of God in our lives to help us to relate to others. There was a time in my life when I had to work closely with two people who seemed always to 'rub me up the wrong way'. Every time I encountered them, whether it was in a work situation, or in church, I always felt irritated. This drove me to seek God. It was during this time that I felt God show me what I have just shared. I worked this through with God and I soon found that the irritation had gone. It was not the case that they had changed because they were still the same, but something had happened in my life and I no longer felt the way I did whenever I met them. I had received the grace of God into my life in order to help me to relate to people who in the 'natural' it would not be easy for me to interact with. Another verse that helps us here is found in Hebrews 12:15. It tells us to make sure that no one misses the grace of God and that no bitter root grows up to cause trouble and defile many. Bitterness so easily creeps upon us that often we do not realise that it

211

is in our heart. Most bitterness occurs in relationships, therefore the scripture tells us that when we miss God's grace bitterness can defile us. The injunction here is to be careful that we do not miss God's grace. At this time one scripture that was a real help to me was Hebrews 4:16 that encourages us to approach the throne of grace with confidence, so that we may receive mercy and find grace to help us in our time of need. Whenever we are in need we can approach God's throne and receive from Him the grace that we need to help us. In line with this I find 1 Peter 4:10 another interesting verse. It says,

> *'that each one should use whatever gift he has received to serve others, faithfully administering God's grace in its various forms.'*

It would appear that there is far more to the grace of God than we would at first believe. It has *'various forms'*. In other words it can be whatever we need it to be. Whatever we need to receive from God, when we come to Him in confidence, it is His grace that we receive. Whether it is healing, salvation, peace, rest, self-control, patience, tolerance, perseverance, or whatever, we can receive it from God's throne.

Another of the areas that I have experienced the grace of God to be of help to me, is when I have travelled overseas with my husband on missions. In many of the countries I have found the culture hard to cope with. Some of the living accommodation has been hard for us who have been brought up in a western culture. There were times when we shared our bed with cockroaches! Beds which have been just wooden slats. Bedrooms which have had no windows or ventilation of any kind. No air-conditioning, in temperatures of well over 80 degrees Fahrenheit. Food that one was not sure was fit to eat. No baths, and toilets which were very unhygienic. I could add many more items to this list. In all these, and more, I have been able to find the grace of God. I count it a privilege to have been able to go to these places and witness just how the grace of God has been there, available to me at **all** times and in **all** situations.

James gives us this lovely insight in chapter 4 and verse 6 of his letter – *'But He gives us more grace.'* More grace! We can never run out of God's grace. Then Peter tells us in 2 Peter 3:18 that grace is something that we can grow in. It would appear that the grace of God is something that grows and matures as our relationship with God develops.

To live a victorious life we need the grace of God to help us:
- in our weaknesses,
- in our relationships,
- in our speech, conversations and communications,
- in our gift and calling,
- in our humility,
- in every circumstance, and
- in order to live a holy life.

If there is any other way that we need His help it is through the grace of God that we will find that help in time of need.

Chapter 42

Overcomers

To live in victory in Bible terms is to be an overcomer. We see this clearly in 1 John 5:4. We somehow seem to miss this positive statement of John's:

*'for **everyone** born of God **overcomes** the world.'*

Often it would appear that we read a 'reverse' version that says 'only some of those who are born of God will be able to overcome.' Or may be we read it like this – 'for everyone who is born of God will only be able to overcome the world sometimes.' A more positive scripture we could not find! The victory we have in Christ will mean that we are overcomers.

Romans 8:37 says that we are not just conquerors but we are **more** than conquerors. What does this mean – 'more than conquerors'? A conqueror is someone who masters, surmounts, and triumphs over. In other words we do not yield to someone who is trying to capture us. We rise above them and do not live under their domination. We are the conqueror, not the conquered. This means that we are living in victory.

I want to look at the book of Revelation, in particular chapters 2 and 3. In these two chapters we have the messages that were given to John for the seven churches in Western Asia Minor. If you read these carefully, you will see that there are two particular things that are included in each of the letters to the churches.

The first is that,

> *'He who has ears to hear, let him hear what the Spirit says to the churches.'*
>
> (Revelation 2:7, 11, 17, 29; 3:6, 15, 22)

Ears to hear! Do we have ears to hear? Are we hearing what God is saying to us, as individuals, and to the church – the Bride of Christ?

The second is that what the Spirit says to all the churches is the same, and it is that,

> *'He who overcomes I will give . . .'*
>
> (Revelation 2:7, 11, 17, 26; 3:5, 12, 21)

Each of the churches, no matter what their particular problem, had the same message, *'He who overcomes. . . .'* God is expecting us to be overcomers. His desire is that we will live a life of overcoming. Not just overcoming Satan, for that has already been done on the Cross of Calvary by our Lord Jesus Christ, but that we should be overcomers in this world, of this world's systems; and be an overcomer in our personal life, by overcoming our natural inclination to sin. Satan, using the will that God had created within him, rebelled against God, desiring to be His equal. Man copied this rebellion and disobeyed what God had said to him. Today sin is still rebellion and disobedience to God. Sin is our own responsibility. We have a free will that God created us with, and which He will never take away. By our will we can say 'No' to Satan's temptation, and 'Yes' to the rule and reign of Jesus Christ in our lives.

A life of victory here on this earth is available to each one of us who will take God at His word; believing what He has said about us; availing ourselves of what He has provided; living in the reality of what He has equipped us with; having faith in who He is.

If we look closely at the things that God says He will then give to those who overcome, we will notice that they all tie up with what Paul and the other writers in the New Testament say can be ours in Christ:

- the gift of eternal life (Revelation 2:7, 11);
- manna from heaven, spiritual food, and a new name (Revelation 2:17);
- a white robe, which speaks of the righteousness we have in Christ (Revelation 3:5);
- authority to rule (Revelation 2:26; 3:21);
- a place in the temple of God, which is the church of God, and therefore a place in His Kingdom (Revelation 3:12).

The important thing for us to do, is to take seriously the injunction that these things will only be given to those who become overcomers. It is therefore important for us to endeavour to live a life in victory. Let me emphasise as I have done many times, that God has done everything He can; He has provided all that we need in order to live a life of victory; all that remains is for us to believe what He has told us, and to receive what He has provided.

My prayer is that what I have written will assist you in your search for God, teach you to build character into your life, and equip you to live in victory.

'He who has ears to hear, let him hear what the Spirit says to him who overcomes, I will give.'

Further Study and Some Suggested Practical Exercises

For those of you who are serious about your relationship with God, and have a desire to build character into your life so that you can live in victory and be effective for the Kingdom of God, I have prepared some practical points for you to follow.

The following is a work sheet and study plan on the fruits of the Holy Spirit. Read through the scriptures and then answer the questions following each group.

1. *John 15:1–8*
    Who is the vine? Who are the branches? Who is the gardener?

2. *Matthew 3:8; John 15:16; Romans 7:4; Philippians 1:11; Colossians 1:10; 2 Corinthians 9:10*
    What kind of fruit should we bear? Why did Jesus choose us? Who do we bear fruit for?

3. *Psalm 92:14; Ezekiel 47:12; Matthew 13:8; Galatians 5:22, 23; Ephesians 5:9–11; James 3:17*
    For how long should we bear fruit? How often should we bear fruit? What kind of soil bears good fruit? How many kinds of fruit should we bear? What helps us bear good fruit?

4. ***Psalm 1:3; Matthew 13:23; John 12:24; John 15:2, 5***
   In what kind of conditions do we need to be planted in, in order to bear fruit? What will happen to seeds in the ground before they will produce fruit? What does this mean for us? What two things should happen to us in order for us to bear fruit?

5. ***Matthew 3:10; Matthew 13:22; Luke 13:6–8; Hebrews 6:8***
   What will happen to us if we do not bear any fruit? What can happen us to make us fruitful?

6. ***Hosea 10:1, 13; Matthew 7:17; Galatians 5:19–21***
   What are the fruits of sinfulness? If we do not like the fruit we are reaping in our lives, what should we do?

In order to discover what gifts and natural talents God has given you may like to do the following exercise:

- Select a few people you are close to; people who you can trust; people who know you really well. It would be good to have among them a leader of your church, a family member, a mature person and someone who you can open yourself up to and be vulnerable with.
- Give each person the following list, asking them to comment about you in each area:
  - what strengths do they see in your life?
  - what do they consider to be your weaknesses?
  - are there any of the fruits of the Spirit evident in your life?
  - are any of the other characteristics we looked at in the second section in your life? (Because they have not read the book it would be good to list them.)
  - what are your natural gifts and talents?
  - do they see any of the spiritual gifts mentioned in the Bible forming in your life?
  - ask them to make any other comment they would like to make with reference to your character and gifts.

- After you have received their replies make some short-term goals. Things that you can do something about and come to grips with on a practical level fairly quickly.
- Make some mid-term goals. Things that will take a little longer to develop.
- Make some long-term goals. Where are you aiming to get to?
- Become accountable to one of the people for the short-term goals to begin with, and as you develop expand to the mid-term and long-term goals.
- If necessary determine what you can do by way of developing the gifts seen in you. In what ways could you start to use them for the benefit of the church and the kingdom of God?
- Is there any training you can have in order to become mature with any spiritual gift seen in your life? If so, make plans to do so under the authority of your church leaders.

If you are one of those people who have found it difficult to hear God, or are unable to rest, do the following exercises:

- Take time to train yourself to be quiet. Set aside, in your diary, a time during this next week when you will stop all activity, be still and teach yourself to hear your own spirit and the Spirit of God. It may be when you have a bath, before you go to sleep at night, first thing on waking in the morning, or maybe taking a walk, but plan a definite time when you will do it. It does not need to be a very long time, to start with – just 5 or 10 minutes. Do nothing during this time. Do not think about writing a shopping list, or think of jobs that need to be done. Do not read your Bible, or another book, do not spend the time praying. Just relax and allow your spirit to be quiet before God. Start an initial commitment to God by praying for His peace to be upon you.

- Start to put the principle of God's Word into action by taking a rest. It may be difficult to set aside a whole day because of family, but at least plan a few hours when you can rest. You may need to begin by repenting before God for breaking His commandment to have a day of rest.
- Evaluate your own life. Have you become too busy to rest? Are you a workaholic? Perhaps you are not aware that you are. Ask your family and friends what they think.
- Take time to evaluate God's call. Has He really called you to do all that you are doing? Don't think that the priorities of last year will continue into the next year. God may have different things for you to do. Re-establish your boundaries and maintain the focus that God has given you. Remember Matthew 11:29–30; His yoke is easy and His burden is light.

The following is a devotional plan for one week, just to help you get started on the road to hearing God, and allowing the scriptures to speak to you. I suggest that you have a pen and paper available each day so you can record what you feel God saying to you. Begin by praying, and opening yourself up to the Holy Spirit, asking for the cleansing of your mind so you can be clear of worldly thoughts to concentrate upon God. Practise being quiet in your spirit so you can hear the voice of God. Clear away anything that you know would hinder you from hearing and recognising God's voice. There are many prayers in the Psalms that can help us to concentrate our thoughts upon God and His word. A good example is found in Psalm 19:14:

'May the words of my mouth and the meditation of my heart be pleasing in your sight, O LORD, my Rock and my Redeemer.'

Further Study and Some Suggested Practical Exercises

Day 1:   Read 2 Peter 1:3-11

Allow the Holy Spirit to speak to you from these verses. Make a note of the things that you feel relevant to your life. Make plans to do something about the things He says to you.

Day 2:   Read Ephesians 4:1–16

Once again allow the Holy Spirit to pin-point specific areas in the passage that need attention in your life. Be positive about what you feel He says and have a goal to do something practical about it.

Day 3:   Read Jeremiah 29:11–12

Allow the Holy Spirit to convey to you God's heart for you as a person.

Write down what He says to you for future reference. Do not confine yourself to just this one scripture. Allow the Holy Spirit to give you other references.

Day 4:   Read Psalm 37:1–11

Meditate on the verses that speak about the things that we have to do.

Day 5:   Read John 17:20–26

Allow the Holy Spirit to convey to your heart just what was in Jesus' heart when He prayed this prayer for you. Write down the things that Jesus said would be ours as a result of Him coming to earth.

Day 6:   Read Romans 8:1–17

Contemplate the things that are mentioned in this passage that we can expect to be in our lives as a result of being 'in Christ'.

Day 7

Today I want you to quietly wait upon God, not requesting anything from Him. Worship Him for who He is.

221

Concentrate on the things that you know about the character of God that you have experienced in your own walk with Him. Let Him communicate to you just what He wishes to say to you. Do not forget – this is a dialogue between you and your Heavenly Father. He has something special He wishes to communicate to you, give Him room to do just that.

Finally as a test ask yourself the following questions. These are just a selection of the questions Jesus asked people during His ministry. Give honest answers, be real with yourself. After you have answered them consider how your answers weigh up with what you feel should be the right answers in the light of what we have shared in this book.

- 'Why do you worry about clothes?' (Matthew 6:28).
- 'Why do you look at the speck of sawdust in your brother's eye and pay no attention to the plank in your own eye?' (Matthew 7:3).
- 'Why are you so afraid?' (Matthew 8:26).
- 'Why do you entertain evil thoughts in your hearts?' (Matthew 9:4).
- 'Why did you doubt?' (Matthew 14:31).
- 'Why are you thinking these things in your hearts?' (Luke 5:22).
- 'Why do you call me, "Lord, Lord," and do not do what I say?' (Luke 6:46).
- 'Why don't you judge for yourselves what is right?' (Luke 12:57).
- 'Why are you sleeping?' (Luke 22:46).
- 'Why are you troubled, and why do doubts rise in your minds?' (Luke 24:38).

The following are some suggestions for you to follow if you are one of the people who consistently have a problem with pressure.

Start by making a note of any habitual sin pattern that you feel you have. This would most likely be in an area of weakness. Each time you come to this weakness consiously ask God for His help, His grace, to overcome. Work at it, do not give up, persevere. Remember being free to fail does not make you a failure!

Those whose problem with pressure is in the area of work, need to seek God for wisdom. Ask for His wisdom on the job that you should tackle first. Make a list of priorities. Fit your work into those priorities. Take them one at a time and finish that before taking the next one.

Also available is Don and Heather Doubles's manual on marriage and family life, *Follow the Maker's Instructions*.

In the foreword Dr Patrick Dixon (ACET) calls the book 'punchy, down to earth, humorous, practical, helpful, and full of inspired common-sense.'

Let God speak into your marriage and family through this inspired book.

On sale at your local Christian bookshop, or at Good News Crusade Bookshop: